FOR THE WOMEN IN MY FAMILY — WHO SEE BEAUTY IN SIMPLICITY, AND HOPE BETWEEN THE CRACKS.

ACKNOWLEDGMENTS

I feel blessed to have been given the chance, once again, to spend my days writing about something that I love. Some say that the process of writing a book is akin to giving birth to a baby, and in some ways I would have to agree. However, I am forever grateful to these wonderful people for making this a far less painful road to travel.

To the visionary team at Murdoch Books — in particular, Kay Scarlett, for the opportunity to express on paper what I feel in my heart and see in my mind. Diana Hill, an angel and a brilliant editor, for her respect and guidance, but above all, her patience! Lauren Camilleri, for capturing with such grace the essence of my words and the beauty in the photographs. Thank you.

To Prue Ruscoe — my friend and ally — whose beautiful, inspiring and haunting images give my words and thoughts their sense of purpose and meaning. And for travelling to the ends of the earth with me for this book — literally! (Where to next, do you think?)

To my friends and colleagues at The LifeStyle Channel — past and present — for providing me with a platform from which I can indulge my creativity and a stage from which to spread the word.

To all of the creative and talented individuals who opened their front doors and very generously allowed us to spend time in, and photograph, their private worlds: Wendy Bednarz, Jennifer and Knight Landesman (and my darling Romaine for the introduction), Nicki and John Zubrzycki, Carl and Alison Ryves, Monica Trapaga (for her home and for her beautiful stores, Reclaim and Reclaim2) and my Shanghai comrades (you know who you are). To my adopted town of Bangalow and its environs, for welcoming us with open arms — and a nice cup of tea! In particular, Karina from The Little Booktree, Tracey, Naomi and Nicole from Lazybones Emporium, Lindy from Palace Antiques and Collectibles, Paul from Country House Antiques (Bangalow and Newrybar), Dave from Nurybah Galleries (Newrybar), Gary and Emma from The Harvest Café (Newrybar) and Leslie and Marina from Red Ginger (Byron Bay).

To my mum, for teaching me that there is strength in self-expression.

And last, but never least — to Michael and our angels, Inez and Joe — mes raisons d'être — for allowing me the time and space to indulge in the things that make me who I am.

sense of style
space

SHANNON FRICKE

PHOTOGRAPHY BY PRUE RUSCOE

MURDOCH BOOKS

contents

06 living space

12 01 the space you're in
HOW DO YOU LIVE? WHAT DO YOU DO TO FILL IN THE
HOURS? WHAT BRINGS YOU PEACE? WHAT MAKES YOU
HAPPY? TO CREATE A SPACE THAT ENHANCES YOUR LIFE,
FIRST YOU MUST RECOGNIZE HOW YOU LOVE TO LIVE

16 reflect
24 breathing space
30 engage
36 move
38 gather
42 be brave

44 02 explore your space
WHICH SPACES GIVE YOU ENERGY? WHICH SPACES DO
YOU FIND COMFORTING? THE FIRST STEP IN DISCOVERING
WHICH SPACES MOVE AND INSPIRE YOU IS TO EXPLORE
THE SPACES AROUND YOU

46 viewing space
50 communal spaces
56 sacred spaces
64 working spaces
68 cleansing spaces

72 private spaces
76 eating spaces
82 storage spaces
84 sleeping spaces
92 entertaining spaces
98 transitional spaces
102 alfresco spaces

106 03 making spaces
TO CREATE EXCITING AND INDIVIDUAL SPACES, YOU NEED
TO IDENTIFY THE KINDS OF ENVIRONMENTS THAT UPLIFT
AND INSPIRE YOU. THEN COMBINE THAT KNOWLEDGE
WITH AN UNDERSTANDING OF THE FUNDAMENTALS OF
INTERIOR DESIGN

110 the layout of space
114 odd spaces
122 placing furniture
124 directing light
132 colour schemes
136 patterning
142 texture
152 collections
156 your space
158 index

page

living space

THIS IS A BOOK AS MUCH ABOUT LIVING AND BEING
AS IT IS ABOUT INTERIOR DECORATION.
IT'S ABOUT CREATING SPACES THAT MAKE YOU FEEL ALIVE.
SPACES THAT EMBODY THE ESSENCE, OR AMBIENCE, OF A HOME AS MUCH AS ITS ARCHITECTURE.
SPACES THAT REFLECT WHO YOU ARE AND WHAT YOU LOVE
AND PROVIDE YOU WITH AN ENVIRONMENT
WHERE YOU CAN CELEBRATE YOUR INDIVIDUALITY AND UNIQUE 'SENSE OF STYLE'.
IT'S ALSO ABOUT DEVELOPING THE CONFIDENCE
AND THE INNER FREEDOM TO EXPRESS YOURSELF, FOR YOURSELF.
WHAT BETTER PLACE TO DO THAT THAN AT HOME — THE ONE PLACE THAT TRULY BELONGS TO YOU.

Creating a stylishly decorated interior is one thing; being able to live and breathe in it with ease is another. In my time as an interior stylist and writer I've seen many homes where the design and decoration are disconnected from the activity and life they are intended to support. Your home's interior should be a participant in your life, not just an 'observer' — it should inspire emotion and satisfy the senses, making living that little bit more comfortable. After all, your home bears witness to so many comings and goings, to so much of the laughter, tears and celebration that make up your history. When you decorate your interior in a way that embodies a true sense of who you are and reflects the life and the energy that pulse within its framework, you are creating a home to nurture the soul as well as provide shelter for you and your family.

One of the most interesting aspects of what I do for a living is that I have a genuine excuse to step into other people's homes and see how they live behind their front door, within their inner sanctum. You can tell so much about a person when you set foot inside their home. Everything — from the colour of the curtains and the knick-knacks lying around, to the atmosphere that emanates from it — reveals something about who lives there: their likes and dislikes, the achievements and other experiences that fill the pages of their lives. It's one of the best ways to really get to know a person and understand what truly motivates their emotions and choices.

Gaining an invitation into such a private world is a privilege — and a rare one these days, with so much of our daily life unfolding outside the home. The day to day of living moves forward at such a roaring pace that our homes have become more of a pit stop than a dwelling place where we can unravel our stresses. What a shame, I say, when home is the one place where we should be free to express ourselves in the truest sense, where we can shed our masks and reveal the reality of our life and loves. Where else can you slow the pace enough to give yourself time to forge connections with the people you most value (including yourself)? Where else can you simply let your guard down and just be … you?

But how do you go about developing such a space: a space that combines individuality with ambience

[SPACE]: 'THE FREEDOM AND SCOPE
TO LIVE AND DEVELOP AS ONE WISHES.'

OXFORD ENGLISH DICTIONARY

and verve; one that's stylish and contemporary, but where you still feel comfortable enough to let your hair down and be yourself? The process of filling your home with the fundamentals can be daunting in itself — taking it one step further to garner even a fraction of individuality and personality can be just too much to cope with. But it doesn't have to be like that. The creation of anything begins with a state of mind. If you are open to the experience of it and allow yourself the time to truly focus, it's possible to create in a way that truly serves your needs. I'm not suggesting that we all possess the breadth of creative talent of, say, Vincent Van Gogh or design guru Philippe Starck; however, I do believe that we all have it in us to create of ourselves, for ourselves.

To begin with, it's important that you become acquainted with some simple guidelines, a design recipe if you like. Understanding basic design fundamentals is an important first step to ensure your space has a firm foundation on which to create effectively. For me, this task can be the most tedious of all, given the sometimes overly theoretical nature of design. So, to make the subject easier to wrangle and to spice up the process a little, I find it best to think about design elements in terms of their 'human' qualities — the character traits that ultimately form each element's distinctive personality. I see colour, for example, as playful, full of energy and cheekiness, the life of the party; lighting, on the other hand, is moody, upbeat one minute, dark and deep the next; proportion is balanced and even tempered … But where does the element of space fit into the equation? I see space as the 'stubborn old mule' of the bunch, a little too set in its ways at times and in need of a good metaphorical shove to get it to move with the times; not completely opposed to change, but definitely requiring some persuasion.

The framework of your space, and its character — orientation to the sun, the amount of light and the connection to the outdoors — can have a huge impact on how you feel living within it. In an ideal world we could all knock out walls, put in bi-folds and punch through some skylights to suit our needs. However, the reality is that many of us can't change the floor plan of our homes without going to great expense. But just because you can't make drastic alterations to the framework doesn't mean you can't influence the space in which you live in a dramatic and exciting way.

This book takes the view that space is much more than just the floor plan of the building in which you live. Space comprises not only a home's walls, floors and roof, but also the atmosphere or the energy contained within that imprint. If you think about space in terms of creating ambience, you'll find that the way you decorate your interior will have more impact on how you exist in your space than anything else. To do this, you need to employ all the design elements from colour to layout: the building blocks that will enable you to create a space that truly complements you.

But before you begin to apply the design theory, you need to work out what kind of atmosphere you'd like to create, the type of energy that reflects an honest sense of who you are. For this, you need a strong connection with yourself, your likes and dislikes. Otherwise it's almost impossible to create a space that you love and that serves you on an emotional level. I plan to take you on a journey of discovery, beginning with you simply getting reacquainted with who you are and how you prefer to live. You may be surprised at what you uncover as you move through the pages and take the time to reflect on your life. You might find you love the upbeat energy of communal spaces, or that you prefer sacred spaces dedicated to solitude and reflection; or a combination of the two. Once you become aware of the spaces that inspire you and the energy that you like to immerse yourself in, it's easier to employ the design basics and make decorating decisions to suit yourself.

Ideally, at the end of your travels you will be ready to create a space that represents your unique view of the world and what you have to offer it. I hope the space you create provides you with a backdrop against which your life experiences unfold with ease. But most of all I hope you have fun with it. The creative process is best approached with a degree of light-heartedness, so try just to go with the flow. If you get stuck, leave it for a while and return to it when your mind is more open. As for all creative pursuits, the journey is as important as the destination.

There is a feeling of freedom that comes when you live and create for yourself. The upside is that you will develop the skills required to create a space that nurtures you from the inside out. The downside is that looking long and hard at yourself and the way you live can be a little uncomfortable. But once you do take the first step, you will discover that the world of design, and all the goodies it has to offer, will be there, waiting for you. The key lies in just beginning.

01
the
space
you're in

HOW DO YOU LIVE? WHAT DO YOU DO TO FILL IN THE HOURS? WHAT BRINGS YOU PEACE? WHAT MAKES YOU HAPPY? TO CREATE A SPACE THAT ENHANCES YOUR LIFE, FIRST YOU MUST RECOGNIZE HOW YOU LOVE TO LIVE.

WE SPEND OUR LIVES MOVING THROUGH SPACES…

Every day, from dawn to dusk, we are perpetually manoeuvring our bodies from one space to another: we go from the bedroom to the bathroom, the house to the garden, the car to the shop, the train to the office — in whichever combination is applicable to our particular situation.

Every constructed space we arrive in is different from the one before. As we travel through each space we observe its layout and respond to the activity taking place within it, instinctively gauging what kind of sensory or physical reactions are required for us to operate successfully within its framework.

As humans we derive a sense of comfort from the definition of space. We create borders and put up fences and walls that slice our landscape into more manageable pieces. Indeed, we function at our best when we impose boundaries on our environment. Boundaries create a framework for our lives, providing a sense of meaning and control, and clearly directing our movements not only through space but also through the stages of our life. In erecting houses, apartment blocks and office towers — spaces upon spaces — we stamp the earth with the imprint of our existence; our buildings, gardens, farms and even our graves are evidence of our participation in life. These private spaces provide us with shelter and security, protecting us and our loved ones from the threat of the unknown and uncontrollable influences that lie beyond our constructed boundaries. Throughout history, we have spilt blood and sacrificed life in the interests of retaining control of the spaces that we consider ours.

Within the cocoon of four walls we have some influence over the energy of existence swirling around us. And when the outside world is operating at odds with our own beliefs, our personalized spaces stand as a reminder to us (and those around us) of who we truly are.

It makes sense, then, given our need for influence over our spaces, to personalize the one space where we do have some control over our life — our home. How you mould your own little corner of the world very much depends on what you need from it. Because every one of us is different, the process will be specific to our own circumstances. It's only when you take the time to contemplate and reacquaint yourself with the workings of your life that you become aware of the kinds of spaces that serve your life best.

THE SPACE THAT SURROUNDS US, WHETHER IN NATURE OR IN THE CONSTRUCTED WORLD, AFFECTS THE CORE OF OUR BEING IN WAYS WE ARE OFTEN UNAWARE OF. IT IS WITHIN OUR HOMES, THE COCOON OF OUR OWN FOUR WALLS, THAT WE HAVE THE MOST INFLUENCE OVER THE ARRANGEMENT AND AMBIENCE OF SPACE.

reflect

I've recently sold my house ... It was a traumatic step for me, for many reasons, but not least of all because in a way I feel as someone might after they've sold off one of their children!

You might think that me telling you a tale (and a rather gloomy one at that) about the space that I have lived in for much of my life is an odd way to commence this part of the book. However, there is a reason for it (which is not just for my therapeutic purposes). It's to show how the spaces in which you spend your life can have a dramatic influence on how you live (and love) your life.

I lived in this particular house — a white, weatherboard fisherman's cottage that I shared with my husband and our two children — for ten years. It was, and is, beautiful, situated in a quaint fishing village, not far from the hustle and bustle of the city but far enough away to provide the sense of inner peace so rarely found in hectic urban centres these days. Much of the cottage is over 100 years old; as in many old houses, traces of the lives and energy of the countless souls who have passed through it remain in every nook and cranny. Judging by the calming ambience flowing through its core, happy times have been had there by many generations. And by us (with the odd grey day of course — I'd be lying if I said otherwise). The house is nestled within the most spectacular natural setting. The canopy of a forty-year-old date palm, which was planted by Emily who's lived next door for sixty odd years, protects the deck from the midday sun, and a luscious pink frangipani overhanging the garden provides sweet smells and visual fodder from the onset of spring until the last days of autumn. The tiny suburb in which it sits is lapped by the ocean and enfolded by a blanket of trees, most of which have been there for centuries. Sounds idyllic, and it is. In fact, if it's possible to have love for a house and the area in which it is situated, in the same way one loves a person, then this would best describe my feelings towards it. This house supported the very essence of who I was and how I needed to exist in this world. A couple or so years into my life there I thought I'd only ever move from the house when my children carried me out in a box.

That was, until a few years ago. I began to notice that the streetscape just beyond our front door was beginning to change. Seemingly out of the blue, we were confronted by the unstoppable construction of high concrete walls and remote-control garage doors. One by one, our placid borders, the low-level stone and timber fences that politely divided us from our neighbours, were being replaced with great speed by impenetrable barriers that seemed to snarl 'Keep out'. What happens to people once their garage doors have gobbled them up? Where do they go, how do they spend their time? Do the spaces they inhabit, beyond the high walls dividing them from the streets, fill their souls with joy? Over the coming days, weeks and months I began to ponder these questions.

The space we live in is a powerful thing, whatever form it takes, and each one of us reacts to our visual landscape in a unique way. Sometimes circumstances force us to live in surroundings that don't completely support us. What do you do when that environment is fundamentally at odds with who you are? In my case, it didn't take much time for me to feel the effects. My body began to ache in ways that I was sure weren't just symptoms of ageing! Breathing became more difficult, and I started to develop odd little ailments that hindered my daily tasks in a quiet, but insidious, way. Mentally and emotionally, I began to feel walled in. Over the course of a few years I felt that my soul had begun to fracture. Watching the spaces around me being carved up and fortified was too much for me to bear. Fancy, feeling miserable in paradise. But I couldn't ignore the fact that a part of me felt like it was dying.

I believe, more so now than ever, that when you are at odds with the environment you inhabit, not just in a superficial way — of course there are always improvements to be made — but in a visceral way, then it's almost impossible to live with a sense of being true to yourself. And so my family and I, with that dictum uppermost in our minds, and with much regret for what had been, decided to give up the beautiful house that was no longer serving our needs. Why should you keep something that makes you feel so unhappy, when another person, with different expectations of their life, could enjoy its pleasures?

With the decision made we packed up our life and moved on. We found ourselves in the only place that someone in need of some real space could head to — the countryside. Now, we live in another small white weatherboard cottage, perched on top of acres of rolling hills without a solid perimeter wall in sight. It too is about 100 years old and accommodates a friendly ghost or three, I'm sure, and we are surrounded by more open space than the eye can cope with. Within a moment of deciding, those niggly ailments of mine began to melt away and my world quickly began to feel just as it should. Will we be here forever? That I don't know. However, the doorway is wide enough for the box that I mentioned earlier, just in case.

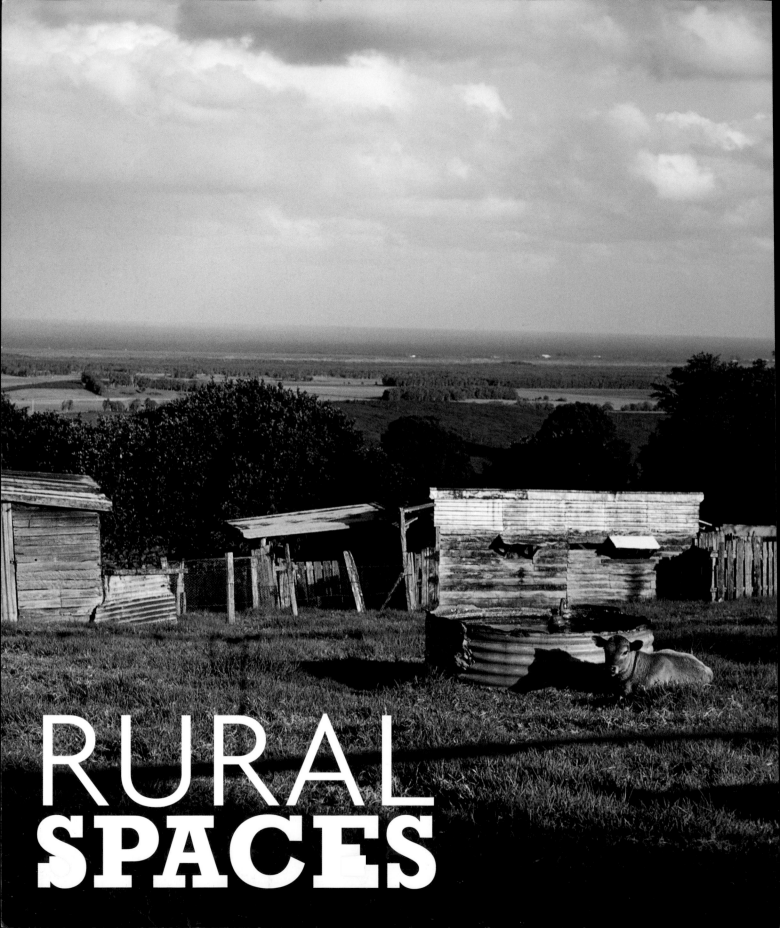

RURAL
SPACES

THE OPENNESS OF THE RURAL ENVIRONMENT PROVIDES A SENSE OF FREEDOM AND HONESTY. HERE, CLOSER TO THE EARTH AND NATURE, WE CAN CLEAR OUR MINDS AND REMEMBER WHO WE ARE AND WHAT WE LOVE ABOUT LIVING.

WHAT IS IT ABOUT A TRIP TO THE COUNTRYSIDE THAT MAKES US FEEL SO FREE? COULD IT BE, QUITE SIMPLY, THAT AMID ALL THAT SPACE — WITHOUT THE CRUSH OF BUILDINGS, CARS, PEOPLE AND CHAOS — WE ARE LITERALLY ABLE TO BREATHE AGAIN? FOR MOST OF US, SPENDING TIME IN WIDE OPEN LANDSCAPES, FREE OF THE VISUAL DISARRAY AND DEAFENING NOISE OF THE CITY, GIVES OUR SENSES A CHANCE TO REGAIN THEIR BALANCE AND PROMOTES A FEELING OF WELLBEING. EVEN JUST A FEW DAYS IN THE COUNTRYSIDE ENABLES US TO ACHIEVE A MENTAL CLARITY THAT HELPS US TO RECONNECT WITH WHO WE ARE AND WHAT WE WANT FROM OUR LIVES.

SADLY, MANY OF US DON'T GET TO SPEND NEARLY AS MUCH TIME IN THE COUNTRY AS WE PROBABLY SHOULD. MODERN LIVING HAS MADE MANY OF US AN URBAN-CENTRIC BUNCH, AND AS A RESULT OUR CONNECTIONS TO OUR RURAL ROOTS HAVE LARGELY BEEN SEVERED. AS AN EX-URBANITE MYSELF, I KNOW I WOULD RARELY GET THE TIME TO TRAVEL BEYOND THE LIMITS OF THE CITY IN WHICH I LIVED. HOWEVER, WHENEVER I DID, I WOULD FEEL A PROFOUND SENSE OF CONTENTMENT AND RELAXATION THAT I RARELY EXPERIENCED LIVING AMONG THE URBAN SPRAWL. IF YOU'VE READ THIS MUCH OF THE BOOK, THEN YOU'LL KNOW THAT I'VE MADE THE CHOICE TO MOVE MY LIFE TO THE COUNTRY — AND I RELISH THE FEELING OF SPACE AND FREEDOM THAT THE CHANGE HAS OFFERED ME. HOW DO YOU REACT WHEN YOU VISIT THE COUNTRYSIDE? DO YOU SHARE THE WONDERFUL SENSE OF GRATIFICATION THAT I FEEL, OR DOES THE VASTNESS OF IT ALL LEAVE YOU A LITTLE TWITCHY, DESPERATE TO RETURN TO THE ACTION OF THE CITY? TRACK YOUR RESPONSES NEXT TIME YOU FIND YOURSELF IN THE COUNTRY. PERHAPS THE FEELING OF SPACE, THE CONNECTION TO NATURE AND THE SIMPLICITY OF THE LANDSCAPE ARE WHAT YOU NEED TO EMULATE IN YOUR HOME. OF COURSE, I'M NOT SUGGESTING THAT YOU NEED TO FILL UP YOUR INTERIOR WITH COUNTRY STYLE FURNITURE TO CONVEY THAT COUNTRY FEELIN' ... UNLESS OF COURSE THAT STYLE TRULY REPRESENTS WHAT YOU REALLY LOVE. RATHER, SEEKING INSPIRATION FROM THE COUNTRYSIDE SHOULD BE MORE OF A LESSON IN HOW

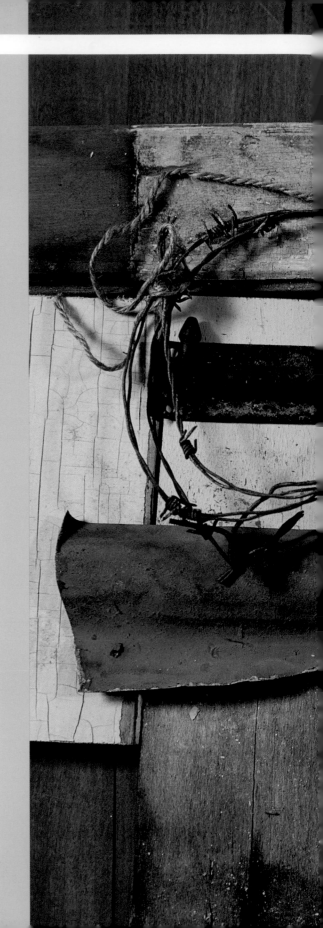

INSPIRATIONAL ELEMENTS:
OPEN HONEST WEATHERED WORN EXPOSED HUMBLE ORGANIC

YOU APPROACH THE FUNDAMENTALS OF DESIGN. KEEP YOUR ROOMS SPACIOUSLY FURNISHED; THAT IS, DON'T OVERCROWD THEM WITH LOTS OF KNICK-KNACKS AND OVERSIZED PIECES, WHICH WILL HINDER YOUR MOVEMENT AROUND THE ROOM. KEEP YOUR PALETTE PALE, BUT INFUSE THE MUTED TONES OF THE COUNTRYSIDE INTO YOUR COLOUR SCHEME — FOR ME, THAT WOULD BE SOFT GREENS, PALE TAUPES AND CHOCOLATES. AND THINK ABOUT USING SMOOTH TEXTURES THAT EMULATE THE SOFTNESS OF GREEN GRASS. OF COURSE, THE COUNTRYSIDE MIGHT WELL MEAN SOMETHING COMPLETELY DIFFERENT TO YOU, DEPENDING ON YOUR LOCATION AND EXPERIENCE. THE IDEA HERE IS SIMPLY TO REGARD IT AS YET ANOTHER FORM OF INSPIRATION TO GIVE YOU A DEEPER UNDERSTANDING OF SPACE AND THE BEST WAY TO FILL IT.

breathing space

Sometimes good things can come from doing nothing, from just being still and allowing the mind to wander. It's the ideal way to begin any kind of creative journey.

Freeing yourself from the monotony of day-to-day living and letting your imagination take you where it pleases is one of the most effective ways to resolve what you need and desire from life. How is it possible to connect with a true sense of who you are if you don't take the time to reflect on all aspects of how you are living? How is it possible to create a space you love living in and conjure an ambience that soothes your soul, if you don't stop to acknowledge the kinds of environments that make your heart sing?

In childhood, we all instinctively appreciate the benefits that come when we use our imaginations. By daydreaming, creating our own alternative worlds, we learn about the complexity of relationships and the environment in which we live. It's how we begin to understand our basic emotions, what makes us happy and sad. I find there is nothing more curious and inspirational than watching my six-year-old son (who is a prolific daydreamer) constructing and play-acting his imaginary game of life. Have you ever observed (or spied upon!) children when they are building their own private world? Whether it's a wooden cubby house, or simply a sheet thrown over a chair, their process of creating and inhabiting secret spaces is simple and pure — the name of the game, though they are possibly not conscious of it, is simply to nurture the spirit. How wonderful to possess the inner freedom to create a world that truly reflects the needs of your soul.

Alas, as we grow into adults many of us lose the capacity to dream. Purpose takes over from play. The drive for success takes over from experimentation. But is it ever too late to begin again?

WHEN YOU TAKE THE TIME TO 'JUST BE', THE WORLD OPENS UP BEFORE YOU AND YOU CAN SEE THINGS THAT YOU NEVER KNEW EXISTED.

THE URBAN STREETSCAPE: A MELTING POT OF COLOUR
LIFE AND ENERGY. THE PULSE OF THE STREET BRINGS

AND CHAOS, THE CITY THROBS WITH ALIVE ALL WHO TREAD ITS PATH.

WE CAN ONLY BEGIN TO FORM AN IDEA OF WHAT WE NEED FROM OUR OWN PRIVATE SPACES WHEN WE MOVE THROUGH THE ENVIRONMENTS SURROUNDING US WITH A DEGREE OF AWARENESS AND CONNECTION TO THEM.

Of course, doing nothing but dreaming does take some discipline — the discipline to switch off from the routine of your daily tasks and to file away your mental 'to do' lists for any length of time. We are a generation of 'doers', after all. Every minute of every day is filled to the brim with action and purpose, so much so that the notion of taking time out to do 'nothing' has, for many of us, become a rather peculiar concept. However, to explore any aspect of creativity, whether it be painting a canvas, baking a cake or in this case decorating your home, it's important to be in the right frame of mind to begin with.

So, give it a try. Find a calming space where you can lie down and relax — it could be that you take to the cosiness of your bed, or perhaps you have a special spot outside in the sunshine. Maybe the bath, where you simply float in the warmth of the water, is the space where you find it easiest to switch off. For me, it's always lazing on my chocolate-coloured linen-covered sofa.

Then, disconnect the mobile. Just ... be ...

Although it may not seem obvious at first, unearthing your ambitions for how you'd like to live, or revisiting old ones, is the first step in trying to connect with the space around you. It's almost impossible to create an environment that serves you and your needs if you haven't established what those needs are in the first place. The most arresting interiors that I have seen have been laid with firm foundations, given a solid 'root system' that captures the essence of those who live there and what makes their lives unique. To create this for yourself, think about your inspirations and your aspirations; what fills you with joy and what makes you feel complete as a person. These desires aren't necessarily elaborate — sometimes the simplest things in life are what we crave the most. If you have children, try to remember what your goals were for your life before they filled it with endless activity and before you became swept up in their vision for living. Is your family unit operating as you planned? How did you see yourself living at this stage in your being? Is your life supporting your ambitions? What is it that brings a smile to your face? What thrills you? What makes you feel at one with yourself? Maybe you feel most alive being on a lazy holiday at the beach; or perhaps it's when you find yourself amid the chaos of a Hong Kong market. Do you operate most effectively surrounded by the bounty of technology or does your heart truly sing when you are connected with the wildness of nature?

Take your time and allow your mind to wander. Pretty soon, you'll find yourself in a place that makes you smile. I promise.

engage

Now that you are still, and your mind is hopefully a little clearer than when you began, it's time for you to look at the world and the spaces around you.

Open your eyes. Let them dart from one corner of your space to the other. Start to visually break down the space into smaller fragments. What does it look like? What does it feel like? Do four walls cocoon you? Is it a small room or an expansive one? Is there much natural light? If you're outside, have a look at and digest the scenery that envelops you. What's going on?

What fills the landscape — is it a natural or an urban environment? How are the elements of space situated relative to one another? Are they huddled together or do they stand alone? Are they harried or still? How does their placement make you feel? Visualize the space you're in as a kind of map or a floor plan and think about how each aspect of that plan relates to the other: the scale, the colours, the light, the atmosphere. How is the space transformed over the course of the day? When is it most alive? Are all of the elements working in harmony, and what kind of response do you have to it, on a sensory, as well as on an intellectual, level? Which elements do you love? Which do you loathe?

Breaking down the spaces around you into more manageable bites, so that you can see how they affect you on a small scale, is a great way to come to terms with the vastness of the subject of space.

THE THINGS THAT FILL OUR SPACES, THE DECORATION THAT WE COLLECT OVER TIME, GIVE THE STRONGEST INDICATION OF JUST WHO WE ARE.

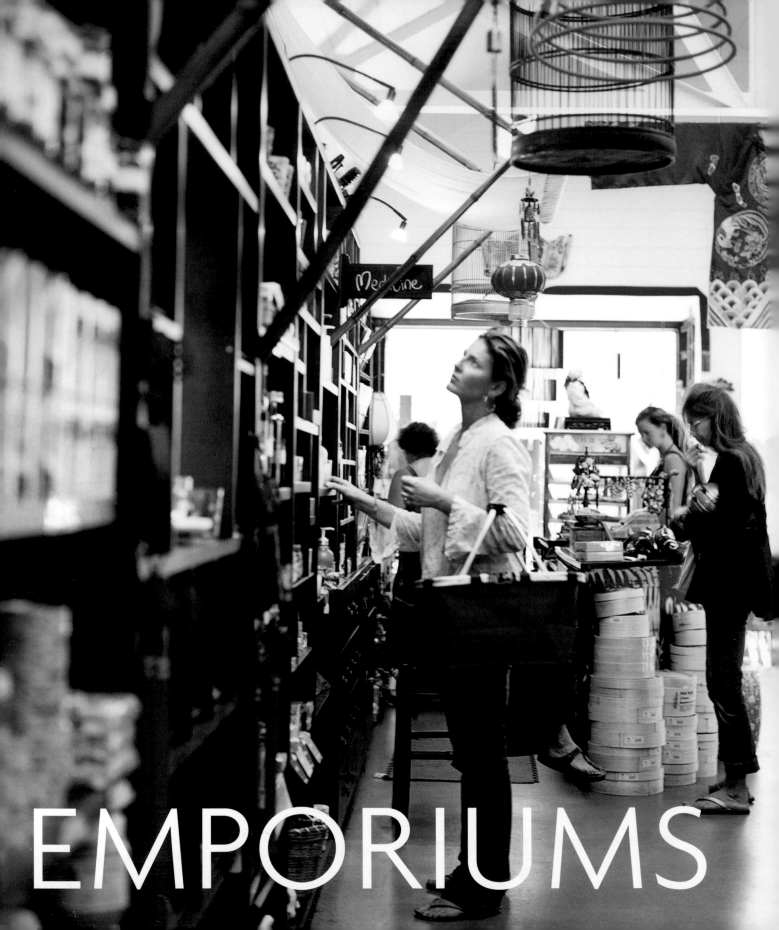

EMPORIUMS

THE SHELVES OF AN EMPORIUM, LINED WITH THE BRIGHT COLOURS AND GRAPHIC FORMS OF A VARIETY OF PRODUCTS — WHETHER FOOD, TRINKETS OR HOMEWARES — PROVIDE A VISUAL FEAST OF INSPIRATION.

EVEN THE WORD 'EMPORIUM' IS ENOUGH TO INSPIRE IN ME A SENSE OF FASCINATION. ALL OF THE POSSIBILITIES THAT LIE WAITING BEYOND THE FRONT DOOR OF AN EMPORIUM (WHICH ACTUALLY IS JUST A VERY LARGE SPECIALTY SHOP), LEAVE YOU FEELING LIKE A CHILD AT THE ONSET OF A VISIT TO A CANDY STORE. ACTUALLY SETTING FOOT INSIDE AN EMPORIUM, REGARDLESS OF ITS CONTENTS, HAS TO BE CONSIDERED ONE OF THE MOST BLISSFUL PASTIMES ON OFFER, PARTICULARLY IF YOU ARE A LOVER OF ALL 'THINGS' (READ: SHOPAHOLIC) AS I AM!

WHILE EMPORIUMS COME IN ALL SHAPES AND SIZES, I'M MOST ATTRACTED TO THOSE FILLED WITH HOMEWARES AND FOOD. MY FAVOURITE HOMEWARES EMPORIUM IN NEW YORK, ABC CARPET AND HOME, IS FIVE OR MORE FLOORS JAMPACKED WITH A MULTITUDE OF HOMEY-STYLE PARAPHERNALIA. WHENEVER I'M IN NEW YORK, I SPEND HOURS GETTING LOST AMONG ALL OF THE WONDERFUL STUFF THAT HAS BEEN GROUPED INTO THE MOST INSPIRING DISPLAYS. THERE ARE GORGEOUS THINGS APLENTY, AND EVEN THOUGH THIS WAREHOUSE IS THE MOST GIGANTIC OF SPACES, THE WAY IN WHICH THE SPACE HAS BEEN DISSECTED INTO SMALL, INTIMATE VIGNETTES THROUGH THE USE OF FURNITURE AND DECORATION GIVES YOU THE FEELING YOU'RE WALKING THROUGH ALADDIN'S CAVE. ALTHOUGH I FIND IT HARD TO LEAVE THERE WITHOUT BUYING ANYTHING, TIME SPENT IN THIS WONDERFUL STORE IS REALLY ABOUT GAINING INSIGHT INTO THE WAY THAT DECORATING CAN TRULY DEFINE THE AMBIENCE OF A SPACE. RED GINGER, AN ASIAN FOOD EMPORIUM IN BYRON BAY, AUSTRALIA, FEEDS MY SENSES (AND STOMACH) IN MUCH THE SAME WAY. THIS WONDERFUL ASIAN FOOD MARKET SPECIALIZES IN ASIAN INGREDIENTS AND OTHER BITS AND BOBS AND IS A VISUAL TREASURE TROVE — THE WALLS ARE LINED WITH ROWS AND ROWS OF GORGEOUS PACKAGES WHICH STIMULATE THE EYE WITH THEIR STRONG COLOURS AND DISPLAY OF BOLD TYPEFACES. THE SPACE ITSELF IS FAIRLY INNOCUOUS — THERE IS NOTHING ABOUT ITS ARCHITECTURE

INSPIRATIONAL ELEMENTS:
CLASHING UPLIFTING INSPIRING RIOTOUS GRAPHIC

THAT SETS IT APART FROM THE REST — INSTEAD, THE LAYOUT, COLOUR AND FORM COUPLED WITH THE LIVELY ATMOSPHERE GENERATED BY THE ORIGINAL AND ECLECTIC DECORATION GIVE THIS SPACE ITS UNIQUE FLAVOUR.

PLACES LIKE THIS ARE A GREAT EXAMPLE OF HOW IT IS POSSIBLE TO GIVE A SPACE, OFTEN AN OVERSIZED ONE AT THAT, AN AMBIENCE AND AN INDIVIDUAL SENSE OF STYLE. AND SO, AS IS ALWAYS MY ADVICE, I RECOMMEND THAT YOU INDULGE IN A DAY OR TWO OF SHOPPING — FOR RESEARCH PURPOSES, NATURALLY. REMEMBER TO TAKE YOUR CAMERA ALONG (AND YOUR CREDIT CARD) SO THAT YOU CAN RECORD ANY HIP IDEAS THAT YOU MAY COME ACROSS. IF DRAWING IS YOUR TALENT, WHY NOT SPEND THE TIME ILLUSTRATING YOUR THOUGHTS INSTEAD? THIS APPROACH WOULD MAKE FOR A VERY DISTINCTIVE INSPIRATION FILE OR MOOD BOARD. YOU NEVER KNOW WHAT GREAT VISUAL STIMULATION YOU MIGHT FIND ALONG THE WAY.

move

How you move through your existing living spaces – can you do so with ease, or is it a struggle? – will give you a sound indication of the types of spaces that best suit your life.

The architecture of a space dictates to an extent how you live within it. But it's not everything. In fact, it's the energy that characterizes a space, the energy transmitted by the activities taking place within it, that has the most powerful effect.

Identify how different spaces affect you by moving through them and consciously noting the reaction you have to each new environment. How do you feel in a space, on an intellectual, above all on a sensory, level? Connect with your senses and trust your instincts; these will give you a clear insight into the long-term effects the space is having on you. I once spent time working in an artificially lit, air-conditioned city high rise, with no view of the outside world: my extreme, negative reaction to this space convinced me that in my home a fresh breeze and a visual connection to nature were essential for me to maintain my equilibrium.

Your response to different environments will give you an indication of the kinds of spaces in which you feel most comfortable. Track your responses. Over time you will see a pattern emerging that will help to guide your choices. I've spent enough time in oversized, open-plan rooms that spill into each other with little in the way of division, to know that the effect leaves me feeling rather like a tiny fish in a very large pond. Perhaps it stems from the fact that I grew up in small houses and apartments and so I react best to the cocooning effect of these spaces. Once you've established the types of environments that make you happy, you can go about using design fundamentals to create a space that you love.

At this point, though, don't think too hard about what you require of your space from a practical perspective (we'll get into that later) — all that I'm hoping you'll achieve here is to gain some sense of awareness of and connection to the everyday spaces that surround you. And remember, the world around us is never, ever still. Even the quietest environments are on some larger or smaller scale in constant motion. Sometimes the environment that suits you best may appear in a fleeting moment. The trick is to see it when it does.

WHEN YOU CAN MOVE WITH EASE THROUGH YOUR SPACE, BOTH PHYSICALLY AND METAPHORICALLY, YOU KNOW THAT THE SPACE IS AN HONEST EXPRESSION OF YOUR SENSE OF SELF, AND YOUR SENSE OF STYLE.

gather

The things we surround ourselves with, the details that fill every nook and cranny of our lives, paint the clearest picture of who we are and how we prefer to exist.

When was the last time that you took a good look at the 'stuff' that fills your life? Those bits and pieces you gather, often subconsciously, that make you feel safe and secure, feed your emotions and soothe your soul. The objects that you are drawn to, often without even realizing it, that give you an insight into what you love and how you would be happiest living. You may find that one particular colour, pattern or form takes precedence over all the others in the spectrum: these elements will help you to build a certain kind of ambience. Look closely, and your things could give you a clue about what kinds of spaces will work for you. My seven-year-old daughter is a bowerbird at heart — she collects everything from bottle tops to ribbons and countless, tiny pieces of paper (in every imaginable colour) which are strewn across floors, shoved into bags and hidden under pillows. Her bed is covered in stickers and the walls of her bedroom are papered in posters of celebrities (much to my despair). Her collections are created instinctively rather than rationally, and it's her heart that guides her choices. Although the mess drives me completely insane at times, I know that these little details soothe her soul. It's the busyness, the jumble, of her things that inspires her and gets her through each day. Take away her collections and pop her into an empty space and she's left devoid of energy and direction. Of course, I hate to think what life will be like in my house when she hits her teens … one thing is for sure — it's going to get messy.

Have a good look at the much-loved objects that fill the corners of your life. These don't have to be expensive gadgets or designer garb. They could be as simple as pictures torn from a magazine that you

'STYLE IS KNOWING WHO YOU ARE, WHAT YOU WANT TO SAY
AND NOT GIVING A DAMN.' *GORE VIDAL*

pin up on your refrigerator, or your collection of ceramics. Do you love seeing your things on display, or do you need your things to live behind closed doors? Look at your possessions objectively. Maybe it's your collection of coloured glass that inspires in you the strongest reaction, indicating a love of vivid colour, clean lines and smooth textures. Or maybe your bowls of shells and pieces of driftwood are what draw your eye most passionately, in which case a plain, neutral palette could be what you need. I find that photographs are often the most insightful tools to use. What do you find when you turn the pages of your albums, which memories evoke in you the strongest reactions? Every picture tells the story of your life. Which story sits best with your vision for living?

You may, theoretically, love the idea of living in a clean, contemporary, ordered space; however, when you do this exercise and work through to the level of complete honesty about your likes and dislikes, you might find that in reality the crazy, colourful and messed-up spaces give you the biggest thrill. Or it could be the reverse — fashion may dictate that wild colour and colliding pattern are the order of the day, but it's the serenity of a simple, uncluttered space that really fuels your spirit. Of course, the trick is to distinguish a fleeting attraction from intense yearning. On the surface you can be a great many things. In my case, one minute I'm an Armani type (clean lines and neutral palette) and then in the next breath it's mixed-up and crazy Versace-style all the way. In reality, though, I think that my style lies somewhere in the middle: just enough colour and clutter to keep the landscape interesting, but not so much that it sends me over the edge. That's just me. Remember, when it comes to your home, there are no rights or wrongs, it's all about unearthing your unique reaction to life and living. So delve into the things that surround you and try to look at your 'stuff' objectively. When you do, you may just find a thread of style emerging.

be brave

As with all creative adventures, it's the fine balance between reflection and action that will get you to the place where you need to be.

Too much thought and no action does not a pretty interior make. Too much action with too little thought will have you going round in metaphorical circles. Take the time to think about what you want and need to achieve from your space before you dive into creating it. However, once you have resolved your aims, reflect no further.

Now that you have cautiously dipped your toe into the process of self-education, and feel more comfortable with the subject, be brave: immerse yourself in all its possibilities. Dabble to your heart's content. Peruse your favourite shops, cafés and restaurants, looking closely at the different colours, patterns and forms that fill each space. How do the elements relate to one another? Are the spaces filled with light or do they spend most of the day in the dark? Is the furniture contemporary? Vintage? Are the fabrics patterned or plain?

How does the space make you feel? Then draw up a plan, develop a mood board or begin a design file and fill it with examples of the things that move you and make you smile. This could be anything from pebbles washed up on the beach to postcards that remind you of your favourite holiday destination.

Take your time. There is no hurry. Live with your ideas for a while before you make any final choices, to be sure that your attraction is not short lived. Uncovering what you love and then experimenting with that reality is a lengthy process, which will always be evolving to some degree. Just as your likes and dislikes will change as you are exposed to new ideas and ways of living, so will your interior — it is a reflection of you, after all. So keep your mind open and explore what's on offer. Once you have conceived your palette, experiment with your choices in a quiet corner where you can make any mistakes with little consequence. Over time you will gain the confidence that you need to delve further into your creation. If you are unhappy with the outcome, go back and alter your choices until you are content with your efforts, bearing in mind that even the most experienced among us suffer an aesthetic hiccup from time to time. It's true that when it comes to creativity sometimes the most enduring creations are born from a 'blunder'.

02
explore
your
space

WHICH SPACES GIVE YOU ENERGY?

WHICH SPACES DO YOU FIND COMFORTING?

THE FIRST STEP IN DISCOVERING WHICH SPACES MOVE AND INSPIRE YOU
IS TO EXPLORE THE SPACES AROUND YOU.

viewing space

Stop and take a good look at the spaces around you, those that you find yourself in every day, and gauge how these different spaces make you feel.

The environment in which we find ourselves day in, day out — home or office or other — affects us in ways we often aren't even aware of. We tend to move subconsciously through the spaces that make up our lives, reacting more to the activity that swirls around us than to the space itself. However, the way a space is structured and decorated can actually stimulate your emotional reaction to it, just as much as the goings-on taking place there. The two work hand in hand. Without activity or purpose, a built space has little meaning — it is simply an empty box. And it works the other way: you need a sympathetic location for any activity you want to perform effectively, or a suitable stage for the sentiments that you may wish to express.

To have an awareness of the spaces around you, first of all you must develop a deeper consciousness of your self. To understand what kinds of spaces you want to create you need a sound sense of how you will exist as a part of those spaces. In Chapter 1 of this book I hope I have prompted you to (re)connect with who you are, with your likes and dislikes, with the things that move and inspire you.

With your needs and desires clearly defined in your mind, it's time to begin the process of developing an active sense of how you would like to 'be' in your home. To do this, I am going to take you through the environments where you would ordinarily spend parts of your day. Nowhere too fancy: just the good old mundane places in which we seem to spend a large part of our lives. My hope is that you will begin to assess and scrutinize what it is about the spaces that does — and doesn't — work for you, from a functional viewpoint, and above all from an emotional or sensory perspective. We can believe, on an intellectual level, that certain spaces are good for us for a number of reasons: because fashion might so dictate, because we may have been conditioned to think so or just because we have had little cause to question the status quo. But you might

THE WORLD PROVIDES US WITH AN INTERACTIVE PALETTE OF SPACE, COLOUR, FORM, TEXTURE AND PATTERN. USE THESE ELEMENTS TO CONSTRUCT YOUR OWN VIEW OF SPACE.

THE INTERIOR SPACES THAT WE CONSTRUCT FOR OURSELVES SAY SO MUCH ABOUT WHO WE ARE, EVERY INCH, FROM THE ENTRANCE TO THE GARDEN, REVEALS SOMETHING ABOUT THE WAY THAT WE EXIST IN THE WORLD.

'WE DEPEND ON OUR SURROUNDINGS
TO EMBODY THE MOODS AND IDEAS WE RESPECT
AND THEN TO REMIND US OF THEM.' *ALAIN DE BOTTON*

find when you get down to the nitty gritty that the way you have been living doesn't really suit you at all; that, up until now, your choices have been guided by factors that don't necessarily reflect your own style. Or you may find that you love your spaces, but that a little tweaking is in order to make them just right.

When you move through the pages ahead, and the different spaces that I outline, look at the individual elements that each space in your life presents to you — that is, the framework, the layout, the lighting, the decoration and so forth — and think about how each of those factors is affecting you on a subliminal level. Then look at the space as a whole and determine whether or not the details are working well together. This process doesn't have to take a lot of time out of your day. A glance around the bathroom while you're brushing your teeth could be enough, or a quick scan of the bedroom while you're reading your book in bed at night will, at the very least, help you to begin the process of connection.

Once you have rekindled a relationship with your space, allow it to develop for a while. There is no hurry: it's important to take as much or as little time as you need, and that will be different for every one of us. Remember that this is all about developing individuality; there are no stock, standard answers and no rights and wrongs. Your reaction to a space will be very different from that of the next person … and that is exactly the point. What we are hoping to uncover and nurture through this process is your unique sense of style.

communal spaces

COMMUNAL LIVING IS ABOUT TOGETHERNESS

Our need to live as part of a community is hardwired into our DNA. Humans have always travelled through life in packs; our links with others ensure our physical and emotional survival. The structure of society and our collective imprint for living have been formed in a way that nurtures our connections to one another. This interaction provides us with the opportunity to think and to feel with a purpose beyond our singular selves, and reassures us that we are not the only ones trying to navigate this vast and crazy universe. Every aspect of our wellbeing is dependent on our relationships with and our support for one another. We find a partner, have families, form friendships, develop communities, join clubs and chat forums, all with the purpose of creating and maintaining connections with other people.

It's important for us to be a part of something that is bigger than ourselves; most of us find it deeply comforting to spend time among a crowd, even if the crowd is made up of complete strangers. Being part of a group of people, particularly those who share our thoughts and ideas about living, gives us a sense of credence and a degree of confidence in the notion that we are not alone in the way we have chosen to live our life. It provides us with a sense of place and a feeling of belonging. When we belong to a group, whether or not the other members are physically present, we can still be alone and still be an individual — but we will never be lonely.

Of course, the need or desire to belong to a community is stronger for some than others. While the buzz of a crowd can be uplifting and invigorating for certain people, it can be downright draining and exhausting for others. And so tracking your reaction to this kind of intense energy is an important first step when determining what type of environments you want (or need) to create in your own home. The last thing that you want is to design a space of such

brilliance and energy that it entices people to drop in at all hours, when all you want to do is cocoon yourself away in a private space meant just for one! However, if the bringing together of many is what soothes your soul and provides you with comfort and contentment, you need to go all out to make allowances for this when you are choosing how to decorate.

DESIGN

Communal spaces are by their very nature exciting places in which to spend your time. They are filled with lots of people who have different lives, different schedules and different energies; creating a space that caters to all of these contradictory aspects can be simultaneously challenging and thrilling. Certain rooms in the house lend themselves to being communal by the natural essence of the activity that takes place within them. The kitchen is the most obvious example. Wherever there is food about, there are people about. Lounge and rumpus rooms, the same.

The layout of any communal space is the most important aspect here — openness in the design and the possibility of connection between those people using the space are integral components. The layout should entice people to come together, so it is best to place your furniture facing inwards to allow for easy eye contact and conversation.

In the living room, for example, place your sofas symmetrically, in an L-shape or a square, to allow everyone spending time there to maintain contact. Create an illusion of connection by using rugs as a kind of pathway between your furniture pieces. A coffee table will work in

[SENSEOFSTYLESPACE]

DESIGN INSPIRATIONS CAN TAKE MANY FORMS, FROM OTHER INTERIOR SPACES TO THE GRAPHIC COLOUR AND PATTERN FOUND LINING THE STREETS.

'FASHION FADES, ONLY STYLE REMAINS THE SAME.'

COCO CHANEL

the same way. The architecture of your kitchen — the way in which it has been designed and installed — will dictate the relationship between the cook and onlookers. Island benches that face outwards allow for easy conversation, which helps to add to the feeling of community in the space. A floating bench will suffice for those kitchens designed without a central island. Fuse your dining room into your kitchen by adding a table and chairs, to create a comfortable nook where people can sit while you are busy preparing the meals.

Of course, open plan spaces are designed and built specifically with connection in mind, allowing you to cook, eat, work and watch television all in the same room. So if a hive of activity is what fuels your fire, go down this path the next time you plan to renovate.

COLOUR

Communal spaces are designed to lift the spirit and create energy and excitement, and so a lively colour palette is the way to go if this is the mood you wish to generate. Stick with strong and vibrant colours to stimulate and promote the feeling of activity in the room. Red is the most obvious example. Its intensity and liveliness are impossible to ignore. Orange works in the same way. Pink is vibrant, although less intense than red or orange; stick with the hotter shades of pink to keep the action going. Yellow, with its sunny disposition, will simply make you smile. Go for the muted versions of all the above colours if you like your action a little less frenetic.

PATTERN

Colliding pattern, coupled with intense colour, is a wonderful tool for promoting the feeling of energy and connection in a room. Use bold, geometric patterns if you need a little contemporary sophistication with your action. Large, painterly patterns, like the ones you find in the Designers Guild range, work to create an energized, vital atmosphere. Small, ultra-busy 'chinoiserie' style patterns, in contrasting designs and strong colours, will really keep you on your toes.

sacred spaces

SOMEWHERE TO FIND YOURSELF AGAIN

We all need a space of our own. A place where we can retreat from society and its unfaltering pace; a place where we can, metaphorically speaking, stop the earth from turning just long enough to let us take a deep breath and reflect on our life and the way we are living it. By definition, sacred spaces are tranquil and meditative places that buffer us from the distraction of the world around us. They enable us to restore our faith in ourselves and in the life we lead by providing a backdrop of stillness and stability. In our sacred spaces we are free to balance our heart with our mind and our physical self with our spiritual self. Sacred spaces help to feed the soul.

The definition of a sacred space is different for everyone. For some people, the more traditional places of worship represent a sacred space. A church, a synagogue, a mosque or a temple is the place where some experience a feeling of wholeness, of being at one with themselves and with the life they have been offered. Maybe you find a sense of balance and completion in a quiet corner of a garden. Or in the dim recesses of your local library, where you are surrounded by walls and walls of knowledge.

If you want to create a home that is a heart-centre, a place that allows you to regenerate your spirit and clear your mind, take your inspiration from other spaces around you that soothe your soul. These may present themselves to you in unexpected ways. You may find that it is your trip by car to the office every day, when you can turn on the radio and switch off from your life for a while, that instils in you the most joy. This may indicate that you need to dedicate a space in your house where you can listen to your music, alone, away from the bustle of activity. Perhaps a trip to a health and beauty spa filled you

BLESSED BE THY HOLY NAME

'YOUR SACRED SPACE IS WHERE
YOU CAN FIND YOURSELF AGAIN AND AGAIN.'

JOSEPH CAMPBELL

with a deep sense of self-connection; this could signify that your bathroom is the space that would allow your mind the most freedom, as a place where you can relax and wash away the stresses of your day. Maybe you were inspired by a visit to a temple while you were holidaying overseas, in which case even just a quiet corner dedicated to meditation and inward reflection could be what your soul craves most. Remember that sacred spaces can be as simple or as complicated as you require. Only you know exactly what constitutes your sacred space.

DESIGN

Architecturally, sacred spaces come in all shapes and sizes — from grand cathedrals to a simple, bare room or the far corner of a garden. There is no particular format, no one floor plan, that defines a space as sacred. Rather, it is the energy within the space, whichever form that space takes, that promotes a feeling of calm, connection and harmony. Having said that, the aspect of a space, its connection with the sun and with nature, will also help promote a feeling of peace and serenity. Proponents of the principles of feng shui believe that the arrangement of your furniture has a great impact on the creation of 'good energy' in a room. That is, the placement of furniture with the consideration of ease and flow of movement in mind is imperative to ensure a feeling of happiness and wellbeing. Sacred spaces should be clutter-free, to facilitate freedom from distraction and agitation and to enable you to switch

off from the world and to channel your thoughts and energy inward. At the end of the day, your sacred space should be a place you can retreat to when you are feeling fractured by life. It should help you to feel like a whole person. Whether your sacred space takes the form of a corner in a room, one room in a house, or the whole house, is up to you.

COLOUR

Sacred spaces are by their very nature calming spaces that allow you to unravel your stresses and clear your mind of the day's events. Although I'm not one for dictating how a particular colour should make a person feel, I do think there are some generalized colour patterns that evoke a universal reaction. In this case, a calming palette of colours will help you to reach the desired feeling of enlightenment, more so than the

warmer end of the spectrum. White is the most obvious choice. Not being a colour, but rather a reflection of light, white is a natural balancer — a promoter of calm and tranquillity. Blue and green also, with their connection to the colours of nature, ease tension and free our minds of anxiety, although paler versions work most effectively. However, if orange is the colour that makes you feel most at peace, or red, purple or yellow for that matter, don't be constrained by the status quo. Remember that, as individuals, we all derive a sense of ourselves from different places. There are no rules. It's all about balance — whichever way you achieve it.

LIGHT

The way in which a room is lit can be an important component when trying to generate a feeling of reverence in your space. Low lighting, by means of dimmers, or even candles, works to block out the mess and the detail of the space around you. If creating a designated space specifically for the purpose of generating calm is just not possible in your house, the element of lighting could be what benefits you the most. In this case, wait until everyone has gone to bed, turn down the lights, close your eyes — and remember to breathe. It's as simple as that.

vaches sous
la pluie

GALLERIES

INSPIRATIONAL SPACES

EXPOSURE TO CREATIVE VISION OTHER THAN OUR OWN, WHETHER THROUGH ARTWORK SCULPTURE OR THE DESIGN OF THE SPACE THAT HOUSES THEM, SERVES AS A PLATFORM FROM WHICH TO BEGIN OUR OWN JOURNEY OF SELF-EXPRESSION.

WHAT BETTER WAY IS THERE TO SEE HOW DIFFERENT STYLES OF DECORATING CAN AFFECT THE LOOK OF A SPACE AND THE WAY YOU FEEL IN IT, THAN VISITING YOUR LOCAL ART GALLERY? BY THEIR VERY NATURE, ART GALLERIES ARE BLANK CANVASES, WITH THE FRAMEWORK OF THE SPACE PROVIDING THE BACKDROP TO THE ART THAT LINES THE WALLS. MOST GALLERY SPACES THAT YOU COME ACROSS TEND TO BE STERILE WHITE BOXES, WITH LITTLE IN THE WAY OF PERSONALITY OF THEIR OWN; IT IS THE COLOUR, FORM AND TEXTURE PROVIDED BY THE ART THAT ULTIMATELY DEFINE THE VISUAL INTEREST IN THE ROOM.

ART IS SUCH A STRONG VISUAL REPRESENTATION OF OUR THOUGHTS AND BELIEFS — IT HAS THE ABILITY TO DEFINE AND EMBODY IN THE MOST VISCERAL MANNER THE WAY THAT WE SEE THINGS, REFLECTING WHERE WE ARE IN OUR LIVES AND WHAT IS IMPORTANT TO US. IN A WIDER SENSE, ART REFLECTS THE LARGER HISTORY OF OUR COMMUNITY AND THE TIMES IN WHICH WE ARE LIVING. THROUGH AN ARTIST'S VISION, WE GAIN A WONDERFUL INSIGHT INTO HOW WE COLLECTIVELY THINK AND FEEL, AS WELL AS HOW WE REACT TO THAT COLLECTIVE OUTLOOK AS INDIVIDUALS.

ALMOST EVERY GALLERY SPECIALIZES IN A SPECIFIC TYPE OF ART, WHETHER PAINTING, SCULPTURE, CERAMICS OR THE LIKE. SPENDING TIME IN A SELECTION OF GALLERIES WILL EXPOSE YOU TO A GOOD CROSS-SECTION OF CREATIVITY THAT WILL INSPIRE YOUR INNER DECORATOR. SO, RESERVE AN AFTERNOON AND DEDICATE YOUR TIME TO SOME GALLERY HOPPING. GENERALLY, THERE WILL BE A SUBURB, OR AN AREA WITHIN A CITY, THAT DEVOTES ITSELF PURELY TO SHOWCASING ART, WHICH WILL ALLOW YOU TO GET AROUND TO THREE OR FOUR GALLERIES IN ONE GO. THAT WAY, YOU ARE SURE TO BE EXPOSED TO MANY DIFFERENT STYLES OF ART, WHICH SHOULD GIVE YOU A STRONG INDICATION OF WHAT YOU DO AND DON'T LIKE. YOU MAY DISCOVER DURING THE PROCESS THAT BOLD ARTWORK WITH STRONG COLOUR AND FORM IS WHAT DRAWS YOUR EYE AND MAKES YOU SMILE. PERHAPS CERAMIC

INSPIRATIONAL ELEMENTS:

TEXTURED EXPRESSIVE LAYERED SCULPTED DIVERSE REVEALING

OBJECTS, THEIR SMOOTH LINES COUPLED WITH ROUGH TEXTURES, ARE WHAT YOU LOVE THE MOST? IT COULD BE THAT MODERNIST WORKS SPEAK TO YOUR LOVE OF CLEAN LINES AND SIMPLE FORM. OR IT COULD BE THAT THE MORE CONVENTIONAL LANDSCAPES ARE FOR YOU, INDICATING YOUR LEANINGS TOWARD TRADITIONAL STYLES. OF COURSE, IT IS POSSIBLE TO LOVE ALL KINDS OF ART — WHY STICK TO ONE STYLE WHEN YOU CAN DIVE INTO EVERYTHING THAT IS ON OFFER? IF YOU CAN TRY TO SEPARATE COMPLETE ADORATION FROM MERE ADMIRATION, YOUR SENSE OF STYLE SHOULD START TO REVEAL ITSELF.

Quarterly Journal
A$20.00 (incl. GST)
NZ$25.50 (incl. GST)

Vol. 44   Summer
No. 2   2006

working spaces

A SPACE TO GENERATE IDEAS AND ACTIVITY

For most people, work is an inevitable part of living. However, gone are the days when a regimented working environment determined how and where we worked. Technology has afforded many of us the freedom to work when and where we want: the home, the local café, even the garden shed are being redefined as office spaces. The nature of my work means that I have no particular daily format or routine to base my working life around. I left office life behind many years ago, after realizing that my productivity actually plummeted the moment I set foot in any high-rise environment. The definition of my 'working space' is a moveable feast. One minute it might be a corner booth in my local café; next it could be my home office. Right now, it's the floor of an empty room, where only my books, magazines, paint swatches, computer and coffee surround me, that encourages the clear thought required to write this book.

Our working spaces should inspire and motivate us — they should help us to generate a flow of ideas and promote ease of activity. They ought to enable us to concentrate effectively and to focus on the task at hand. What is considered an effective working space will be different for each one of us; however, at the end of the day, a working space should be a place where we are happy to spend our time — given that much of our time is taken up with working. The

reality of modern living means that we all need to amalgamate some degree of working environment into our homes, even if that space is used for household management tasks like paying bills, making phone calls and general organization. But the parameters of what makes a space successful for working are the same regardless of the work being performed there, so when integrating a space like this into your home it's important to track what kinds of spaces inspire a feeling of motivation and clear thought. You may find that, in fact, you do need a degree of regimentation and structure to enable you to complete the tasks required, and that an orderly space, one with a traditional office format, is what you need. Perhaps you react most intensely to a colourful environment? If so, you need to infuse a bright palette into your home. Or you may feel motivated by nature; if so, a meditative palette and a connection to the outdoors could be what you need.

Once again, the key is to take note of the types of working environments that stimulate your enthusiasm and excitement. Of course, your space must also be comfortable — warm, cosy and enticing enough to prompt a desire to spend time there making your living.

DESIGN

The design of a working space is guided ultimately by the space you have to dedicate to it. For some, that may be a whole room in a house, for others, a pokey corner of the kitchen. Regardless of size and dimensions, all working spaces need to be functional and organized spaces to some degree. It's therefore important to integrate as much storage — that is, cupboards, filing systems and cubbyholes — as you require to be effective and organized. Once you have the systems in place you are free to create an inspiring, individual space in the same way that you would do in any other part of the house. If a connection to the outdoors is important to you, orient your desk towards the window. If this is not possible, pin pictures from magazines of gardens and nature around your desk to remind you of what you love. If the formality of a desk doesn't suit you, an oversized armchair, where you can sit with your laptop in hand, could be a more motivating arrangement. Generally speaking, it's important to have a working space located away from the other goings-on in the house, so you can become fully absorbed in your achievements. In which case, the garden shed could be just the place for you.

[SENSEOFSTYLESPACE]

DESIGNING A WORKING ENVIRONMENT THAT STIMULATES IN THE PERSON USING IT THE DESIRE AND MOTIVATION TO ACHIEVE, MAKES THE PROCESS OF WORK — AN UNAVOIDABLE NECESSITY OF LIVING — THAT MUCH MORE ENJOYABLE.

COLOUR

The colours that you choose to work around should promote a feeling not only of enthusiasm and motivation but also of clarity and clear mindedness. The two need to go hand in hand to ensure productivity. Is it the cheerfulness of yellow, perhaps, with just enough oomph to get you moving, but not enough to send you crazy, that provides that balance for you? Perhaps it is pink, which is simultaneously exciting and soothing. Maybe it is good old office grey that allows you to switch into work mode most effectively. What is wonderful about creating an office environment in your home, as opposed to out-of-home work spaces, is that you are free to experiment with ideas and colour to find exactly what works for you. You may just discover a part of yourself that you never knew existed before.

DETAIL

For me, it is the detail on my office desk (read: clutter) that most inspires productivity. Although I'm sure that you won't find a manual for living that instructs you to fill your life with clutter, I find that it's one of the best ways to get my creative juices flowing. Spools of ribbons, books, magazine clippings, jars of buttons, postcards and so on, all stacked up in not-so-neat piles that beg me to leaf through them, are strewn from one end of my desk to the other. They are the things that I love; the things that simultaneously motivate and soothe me. Although there is a fine line between a little clutter and complete disorder, I find that treading that path is what keeps my enthusiasm for work up and running. What are the details that motivate a desire for work in you? It could be as simple as a photograph of your family placed on your desk, or a library of books on the shelves, or maybe clippings from magazines of the places you intend to travel in your life.

'IF YOU CAN JUST BE YOURSELF THEN YOU HAVE TO BE ORIGINAL BECAUSE THERE'S NO-ONE LIKE YOU.' *MARC NEWSON*

cleansing spaces

TIME ALONE TO REFRESH BODY AND SPIRIT

What a pleasure it is to spend time bathing, to sink into and be caressed by the warmth of water. I find that time in the tub is one of living's most satisfying luxuries — it's time we spend alone, after all, a rare commodity in this communal world, particularly if you live in a household full of children. But it's also an opportunity to free our mind, to unwind physically and to reconnect with our souls and our heart. Allowing ourselves the time to bathe gives us a chance to stop, to think, to release our bodies from cumbersome everyday aches and pains. Its effects are pure bliss — there's nothing quite like the ritual of bathing to cleanse your spirit and calm your inner self; sloughing off the residue of daily life helps us to feel renewed and ready to take on whatever things life throws our way.

What kinds of cleansing spaces induce the feeling of calm and relaxation in you? Which tantalize the senses? Is it the purity of a white-tiled room or perhaps something more hedonistic, something more tactile and sumptuous? At the end of the day, a cleansing space should be designed in

'WHAT YOU CAN DO, OR DREAM YOU CAN DO, BEGIN IT! BOLDNESS HAS GENIUS, MAGIC AND POWER IN IT. BEGIN IT NOW.' *JOHANN WOLFGANG VON GOETHE*

a way that simply makes you feel good. It should ignite all of the senses, while inducing a feeling of quiet and tranquillity. If you can, it is a good idea to spend time at a health spa or bathhouse, to inspire a connection with the kinds of cleansing spaces that make you happiest (and make you feel completely indulged in the process). There are many quirky ideas you can glean by doing your research. An outdoor cleansing room, where you can be connected to nature and the freshness of the air, could be what stirs the strongest response in you. Or a sunken bath, filled to the brim with warm water and aromatic oils. The simplicity of a room lit with the soft glow of candles could be all that you need. Turn to other cultures and their bathing rituals as a guide: the earthly simplicity adopted by the Japanese, or the sensory onslaught preferred by the Swedes. Whether you do your research on site, or through books, magazines, film or television, look at the detail in each space presented to you and isolate the elements that produce the atmosphere you want to recreate in your own home. It doesn't need to be complicated. Sometimes it is something as simple as the smell of your favourite scent that makes you feel complete.

DESIGN

Not often do we get the opportunity to design our bathrooms from scratch, unless of course you are fortunate enough to be building a home that suits your specific needs. However, that doesn't mean you can't create a beautiful space to bathe in. If you are unable to change the floor plan of your bathroom but still want to personalize the space, retiling can achieve your aims most effectively. There are so many options to choose from, depending on your taste. Spending time doing your research, perusing tile shops and bathroom showrooms, will give you an important insight into how you feel among certain colour schemes and textures. You may find that highly glazed mosaic tiles in bright colours are what you want; or perhaps something more earthy, more textured, brings you closer to a connection with your unique sense of style. Maybe you respond to the roughness of bare concrete, tinted a muted blue or green. It is all a very subjective process. If major work is not possible, because you are renting

IMMERSED IN A SOOTHING, WATERY ENVIRONMENT — A BATH, A POOL, THE SEA — WE CAN CENTRE OUR MINDS AND WASH AWAY OUR STRESSES.

or simply can't spare the funds, use decoration to move you closer to the kind of space that you want. Shower curtains, candles, bottles of bubble bath, fluffy white towels and stacks of soap all work to soothe the soul. The trick is to keep clutter hidden, so that your eye is not drawn to mess. Remember, the idea here is to allow your mind some time out — and so your bathroom should be a shrine to all things gorgeous and aromatic.

COLOUR

I love colour in the bathroom — for me there's nothing more clinical and cold than an all-white space. Although a white space looks clean, which is a bonus in a cleansing space, it leaves my soul feeling rather empty. Gentle blues and greens (nothing too disco!) are what help me to unwind most effectively. That's just me. Friends of mine have a bathroom lined head to toe in bright orange mosaic tiles: they find the passion and energy of the orange are what get them going every morning. What do you want from your cleansing space? Do you require a place to unwind, or are you seeking a place to kick-start your energies? Only you know what works for you.

LIGHT

Illumination is one of the most effective tools you can use when trying to create a specific ambience for your bathroom. If you are someone who doesn't like to spend too much time languishing, then bright, efficient light which helps you on your way could be your preference. If you are the type who likes to while away long hours in the bathroom, then soft, dim lighting will aid your relaxation the most. I find that candles, preferably en masse, are what do the trick for me. Surrounding my bath with an abundance of scented candles is all that I need to really get me in the mood for relaxation. The bonus of candles is that the gentle glow hides all of the nasty problems of wear and tear that are inevitable in a space that has such a high degree of usage. The last thing that you need when trying to empty the mind is to see all of those little jobs that need doing.

private spaces

HIDE AWAY FROM THE WORLD AND REJUVENATE

Sometimes we just need a place to hang out, somewhere to tinker and do those things that keep us interested in living. A private space where, depending on how you are feeling at the time, you can potter around doing everything, or nothing. A space that you can escape to even if only for a short time so you can touch base with a true sense of who you really are. In our private spaces we should be able to spend time alone and pursue our interests without the risk of any interruption.

For many men, a private space often takes the form of a garage or a garden shed — a place that gives them a legitimate excuse to while away the hours doing whatever their heart desires; a place where they can spend time with their own private thoughts and accomplish something grand ... or achieve nothing at all.

I find that as a woman it is often harder to drum up such an area — somewhere I can reserve just for myself — particularly because there are kids about; however, I would recommend to anyone that if there's space to spare, reserve it just for yourself. A private space could take the form of a sewing room, a reading space or perhaps an art studio, depending on where your interests lie. I find my home office gives me a legitimate excuse for time out. My office space is the one place in the house where I can lock the door and spend the time that I need fulfilling my interests — whether it be flicking through magazines, looking through paint swatches, chatting on the phone or reading a novel.

A private space should be a comfy place that inspires you to chill out for long periods and encourages you to get lost in your hobby. These spaces should also be a reflection of you as an individual — not the rest of the family — and so it's

'EVERYTHING STARTS AS SOMEBODY'S DAYDREAM.'

LARRY NIVEN

important to approach decoration with your specific interests in mind. If fishing is what stirs you, cover the walls in as much fishing paraphernalia as you would like. If embroidery is what takes your fancy, frame your favourite pieces and line the walls with them. Regardless of how peculiar your interests are, your private space is the one place where you can unleash those interests with little chance of inviting ridicule or unwanted consequence.

So … what are your interests, the things that define you beyond what you do for a living and beyond your role as somebody's mother … father … sister … brother? It's easy to forget about having hobbies these days, as so much of our time is taken up with working and keeping up with the day-to-day stuff. But take your mind back to that period in your life when you had time to spare. How did you spend that time? What were the things that really caught your interest before paying the bills became the priority in your life?

Sometimes it's hard to remember just who you are and what you love; however, if you spend enough time in your own private space, you just might reconnect with exactly who you used to be!

DESIGN

Private space is your own space, a place where you really can unleash your loves with abandon, regardless of how odd that passion might seem to others. However, regardless of the kind of activity in which you plan on indulging, it's important that your private space is first and foremost a comfortable space. With this in mind, a good, comfy sofa should be the first item you move in. Of course, this doesn't have to be the latest, grooviest sofa on the market; in fact, sometimes that old favourite, regardless of how worn in it is, will create the most relaxed atmosphere. Once the sofa is in, line all of the walls and all of the surfaces with the things that make you feel complete, the things that bring back memories of all of those achievements from way back when that have defined who you are and how you approach living. Trophies, ribbons, books, stamps, balls of wool, swatches of fabric, piles of magazines, letters from friends (or lovers), photo frames, your favourite tea cup — these are the things that really make a private space … your space.

eating spaces

SHARING FOOD IS AN EMOTIONAL EXPERIENCE

You'll always find me in the kitchen at parties. In fact, you'll always find me in the kitchen at any time of the day (or night). The kitchen is the heart of the home; wherever there is food about, there are people about. Is there anything more satisfying than opening a fridge that has been stocked with the results of the weekly shop? Perhaps only the wafting aroma of dinner simmering on the stove. Eating a hearty meal fills most of us with joy and makes us feel complete — literally, from the inside out. Eating is such a joyous pastime: it brings people together and so provides a backdrop against which we share our lives and our loves with those we hold dearest. What could be more fulfilling than a communal table laden with the spoils of a trip to the market, and a group of good friends to share them with? A good meal (and a glass of good red, of course) can bridge the gap between ages, cultures and demographics. After all, we all need to eat, regardless of who we are and where we come from — it is one of our common denominators. Ah, food … is there anything more glorious?

Eating spaces are a shrine to the preparation and consumption of food. The design of your eating space (whether the kitchen or dining room) and the atmosphere that emanates from the design have a great impact on the way you enjoy eating and enjoy sharing the experience of eating with others. If

eating means more to you than just the process of sustaining yourself physically, then creating a space that allows you to indulge yourself emotionally is essential in your home.

It makes sense, when sourcing inspiration for your domestic eating spaces, to look to those places outside the home that are drawcards for the hungry droves in search of a good feed. What is it about your favourite eating places that keeps you coming back? Is it simply the food? Maybe it is more about the atmosphere, perhaps the space's aspect to the sun, or the sense of community? Or maybe it's the seclusion, the opportunity to hide in a dark corner and take the time to contemplate living. Perhaps the deep, comfortable sofas are what you love the most — or the ultra-modern décor? Looking to these environments — those you continually return to — is a good place to start when trying to define the kinds of spaces that you hope to emulate in your home. My favourite spaces are light and breezy, but at the same time bustling with all types of people from all types of places. 'Bills' restaurant in Darlinghurst, Sydney, is one example that I turn to in search of inspiration. The open-plan space, which connects the kitchen to the eating area, gives me the feeling of being in a home kitchen — although a rather glamorous one. Over-sized communal tables ensure that everyone who frequents the space feels a sense of connection, even if it is just through eating the ricotta pancakes. The design is simple so as not to compete with the food, and the atmosphere upbeat but laid-back. This is exactly the feeling that I like to create in my own home. You may prefer a little more drama in your space: maybe a more elaborate French-style kitchen, complete with chandelier, could be what complements your food fetishes.

DESIGN

These days, with open-plan living, we often eat in, or at least close to, the kitchen. Kitchen design is therefore an important component when you're trying to create the type of atmosphere you prefer for your eating space. The layout, the choice of cabinetry, tilework and so on are what will really stamp your space with the energy you are after. An all-white kitchen, with marble benchtops and little in the way of decoration, is modern and contemporary and a popular choice in recent times. However, this type of space is more about a quick dip in and out rather than a 'slow food' kind of environment. The more decorative your kitchen becomes, the more homely it becomes. Spanish style tilework on the floor or around the splashbacks sets the scene for a more communal, more family-like, environment. Of course, we don't all have the opportunity to dictate the style of our kitchen, but it is still possible to create a space that you love eating in. Paint is of course the most glorious tool to use; its masking qualities can turn even the drabbest environment into a shrine for all things lovely. White is the most obvious colour (but a little tricky to keep clean); however, the kitchen is a wonderful place to experiment in because of its smaller proportions, so why not be bold with a bright blue or even a hot pink, if you dare?

DECORATION

It's often the simple things that you've used to decorate your interior that encourage the strongest reaction. In the case of your eating spaces, the plates, the bowls and the cutlery, more than anything else, will evoke the kind of feeling you are after. Food tastes so much better when it is being eaten off beautiful crockery, even if the dinnerware is plain and white. If you offer your eating space nothing more than a beautiful plate, you will find this simple gesture can have the most resounding effect. The purity of white is a favourite among the professionals who want the food, not the plate, to be the star. The glimpse of more elaborate dinnerware, however, could fill your soul with joy and bring a smile to your face. Beyond your dinnerware, a good table and comfortable chairs go a long way towards creating atmosphere in your interior. Upholstered chairs, in soft textured fabrics, will see you savouring the moment long after you have finished your meal; upright, plastic chairs (à la Philippe Starck) will cut your dining experience short — simply because you'll be left with a numb derrière! So be sure to choose carefully.

THE RITUAL OF SHARING GOOD FOOD BRINGS PEOPLE JOYOUSLY TOGETHER.

storage
spaces
DECLUTTER YOUR HOME, CLEAR YOUR MIND

We are a generation who love our storage. There's something deeply satisfying about giving our collections (read: clutter) a home, somewhere out of the way or concealed from view. On the surface of it, storage simply makes for a tidy house, but storage is actually more about the desire for order than anything else. When our house is organized, with all the clutter out of the way and out of mind, we function more effectively. Storage helps create ease and flow in the home; it keeps our mind clear and compartmentalized, so we can get on with our daily tasks without too many obstacles. When all your things have a home, that's one less thing to worry about in your busy day.

Thanks to the likes of IKEA and the rest, these days our storage options are numerous: everything from a plastic tub in the bathroom through to whole rooms devoted to storage. It's important to think about your storage needs as more than just a trivial indulgence. If you have ever lived in a house without enough storage (which I am presently doing), you'll know what a complete nightmare it is when there is not enough space in which to hide your things. Of course, the need to hide your possessions away will be different for everyone. Some among us literally can't breathe in a house full of clutter — if this feels familiar, your storage needs will be considerable. Then there are those who don't mind a little mess around the place — it works as a constant reminder of the life that we are living. Then there are those who simply can't live without their clutter — it makes them feel alive, and keeps them in touch with who they are.

Identifying your storage requirements is an important first step when decorating your home. To do this, it's important to ascertain just how much you need to interact with your 'things' on a daily basis and just how important your 'things' are for your vision for living. We are all different in this regard. As a self-confessed hoarder, I say that there shouldn't be any shame attached to those among us who are clutterbugs. So if you can stand it, bring on the 'stuff' of living and let it loose among your décor! That's what decoration is all about, after all.

OUR PLACES OF REST, OUR SLEEPING SPACES, ENCOURAGE THE RENEWAL OF ENERGY AND REBALANCING OF THE SPIRIT ... DESIGN YOUR SPACE IN A WAY THAT PROMOTES THE DEEPEST SENSE OF CALM AND RELAXATION.

sleeping spaces

ROOMS FOR RESTING, REGROUPING, REVIVING

Nothing beats a good night's rest. Getting enough sleep — and the right kind of sleep — makes us feel refreshed, restores our equilibrium and gives our bodies the energy needed to get on with our daily toil. The experience of not getting enough sleep, even for just one night, is all that's required to alert you to how important it is, as any new parent will tell you. After-effects like an inability to concentrate, physical anxiety and a general feeling of mental haziness make the process of living just so much harder to deal with.

Not all sleep is created equal, and to guarantee that you get the right type of sleep — the deep, restorative kind — you need to ensure that all of the elements are in place. A good bed, of course, is the most important ingredient here. Nothing else that you do to your sleeping space will create the effect that you are after if your bed isn't working for you. So do your research, and investigate which kind of bed is best for your physiology. It's a personal thing, but whatever you do, make sure to invest in the best that you can afford. You can decorate to your heart's content, but a beautiful bedspread will not prevent the backache caused from sleeping on the wrong kind of mattress.

Once this practical aspect has been sorted, it's important to identify the type of environment that most effectively promotes the desire to rest. Do you need a dark, quiet haven to induce a feeling of calm; a space with limited natural light and deep-coloured, womb-like walls? Or is the opposite best for you, a light, airy space, with billowing white muslin curtains and crisp, white bed linen — the kind that is reminiscent of holidays by the beach?

Of course, exposing yourself to different kinds of bedrooms isn't always that easy. After all, the

'IT TAKES A LOT OF TIME TO BE A GENIUS, YOU HAVE TO SIT AROUND SO MUCH DOING NOTHING, REALLY DOING NOTHING.' *GERTRUDE STEIN*

bedroom is a sacred space for many people, and getting access to different types of bedrooms is generally an invitation-only affair. Our holidays are one way that we can get first-hand experience of sleeping in someone else's bedroom. Time spent vacationing in a hotel or in the holiday house of a friend could give you some indication of the best environments for you to rest in. For me, the light-filled spaces found in houses situated by a calm sea represent my ideal inner sanctum.

Perhaps you need to think about your inspiration in a less literal way. Which environments evoke in you the deepest sense of quietness and peace? You might feel most relaxed when you are picnicking in the park or while you are lazing on the fine sand of a quiet and secluded beach. Look to the layout of these spaces: are they open and wide, or small and cosy? What about the colour palette? Do the clean, crisp colours of the sea and the sand make you feel at one with who you are — or do you react more to the deep green of the trees and the rough textures of the grass underfoot? If you feel most rested in the quiet of a dark movie theatre, that would indicate your need for a total blackout to ensure your best rest. Again, it's important to think beyond the square when looking for inspiration. Sometimes the best decorating ideas creep up on you without you even knowing it.

FUNDAMENTALS

As I mentioned before, it is by getting the fundamentals of your sleeping space right that you will achieve the deepest sleep. Ensure that your mattress is made for your body and its individual needs. A too soft — or too hard — mattress will almost certainly mean that you don't get the rest you require.

Beyond the mattress, bed linen will help to promote a good night's sleep. Although colour is an important element here, really it is the texture of your bed linen that you should be focusing on the most. You'll know only too well when you are at odds with the texture of your bed linen … just check the neatness of your linen once you've awoken. If it is knotted, twisted and kicked about, perhaps you need to rethink how your linen feels to the touch. Natural fibres — cotton, linen, silk and the like — are the best choices, as they assist airflow and keep your body cool. And of course, they feel wonderful on the skin. Avoid polyester even though it creases less, and therefore decreases your ironing load. Your skin will thank you for it.

DECORATION

Once your fundamentals are in place, it's time to think about the decoration. Ideally, spaces for sleeping should be free of clutter to allow your mind to be lulled into a deep sleep. Computers, paperwork, piles of washing, all the things that represent your daily toil, should be banished from your bedroom and allocated to another area of the house. If space constraints prevail, then partition your work from your sleep with a curtain or screen of some kind. Then dedicate your decoration to expressing the side of yourself that you wish to unleash. Remember that, in general, your bedroom is just for you and those who share your bed, and so it is a wonderful opportunity to experiment with different styles and colours that perhaps you are too nervous to try in other areas of the house. If a dark, moody boudoir is what gets you going, then go for it. Hot pink on the walls perhaps? Why not? Wild, tribal combinations of colours and patterns may be what you need to connect with your inner self. Or a meditative palette of all white could be the thing that you need to reclaim those zzzs.

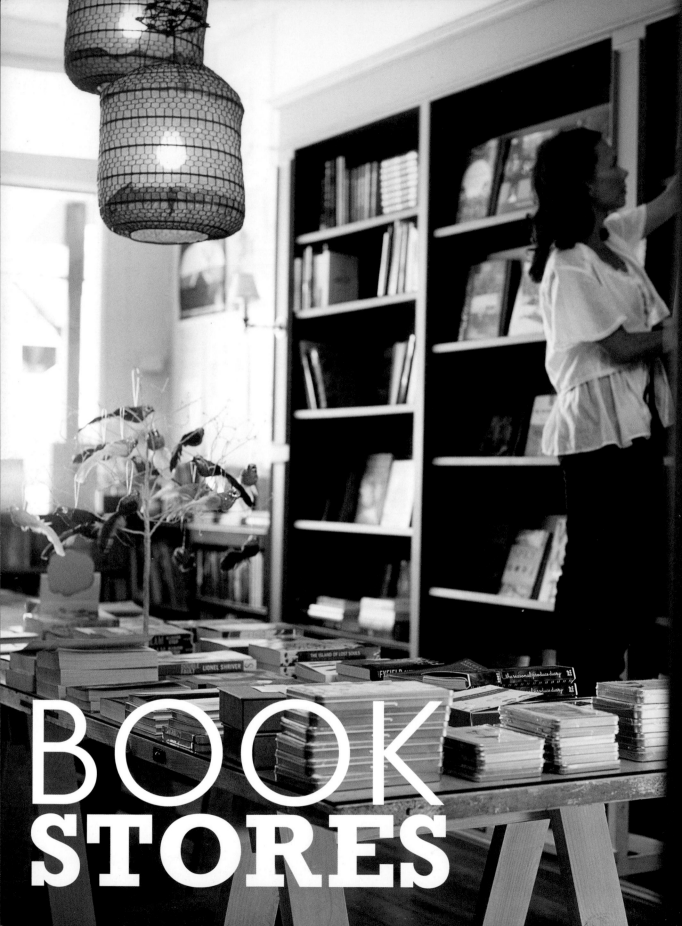

BOOK
STORES

DRAW ON THOSE RECORDED EXPERIENCES THAT BEST SUPPORT YOUR OWN VISION FOR LIVING.

DO YOU

SPEND YOUR WEEKENDS, AS I DO, WHILING AWAY THE HOURS PERUSING THE LADEN SHELVES OF YOUR FAVOURITE BOOKSTORE? IF YOU DO, THEN YOU'LL KNOW THAT SPENDING EVEN A MOMENT AROUND BOOKS, PARTICULARLY IN A SPACE THAT IS FILLED TO THE BRIM WITH THEM, CAN BE ONE OF THE MOST FULFILLING AND RELAXING WAYS TO PASS THE TIME. BOOKSTORES ARE BEAUTIFUL PLACES: QUIET, WITH A SENSE OF SERENITY AND GRACIOUSNESS. YOU CAN BE IN A BOOKSTORE WITH MANY OTHER CUSTOMERS AND YET, WHEN ROAMING THE AISLES, YOU CAN FEEL LIKE THE ONLY PERSON WHO EXISTS IN THE UNIVERSE. BOOKSTORES PROVIDE THE BACKDROP THAT ALLOWS OUR IMAGINATIONS THE FREEDOM TO ROAM. THEY OFFER US THE OPPORTUNITY TO TRAVEL TO FAR-OFF PLACES, TO DELVE INTO MANY DIFFERENT WORLDS AND TO BE A PART OF SOMEBODY ELSE'S STORY FOR A WHILE. IN BOOKSTORES WE CAN SUSPEND REALITY, EVEN JUST MOMENTARILY, AND WE CAN BE TRANSPORTED TO A PLACE IN TIME THAT WE COULD NEVER IMAGINE VISITING IN OUR REAL LIVES. FOR A MINUTE OR TWO YOU COULD BE RIDING AMONG THE CLOUDS WITH HARRY POTTER, OR DEVISING A FEAST FOR YOUR FRIENDS. YOU COULD EVEN BE LEARNING HOW TO GO ABOUT DECORATING YOUR IDEAL INTERIOR SPACE.

SO, WHAT IS IT ABOUT BOOKSTORES THAT MAKES US FEEL SO PEACEFUL, SO TRANQUIL? SURELY IT IS NOT JUST THE ARCHITECTURE OF THE SPACE THAT DRAWS US IN? EVERY BOOKSTORE POSSESSES ITS OWN UNIQUE LAYOUT, NO TWO ARE EVER ALIKE. IT COULD BE THAT SPENDING TIME IN THE PRESENCE OF KNOWLEDGE NURTURES OUR SPIRIT, AND THAT WITH THIS CONNECTION TO THE SPIRIT COMES A SENSE OF PEACE. PERHAPS BEING AROUND ALL OF THIS WISDOM HUMBLES US, BRINGING US BACK DOWN TO EARTH. OR PERHAPS BEING AROUND ALL OF THOSE BOOKS INSPIRES IN US A CURIOSITY FOR LEARNING, A THIRST TO UNCOVER NEW WAYS OF THINKING AND SEEING.

NO MATTER WHETHER THEY ARE LARGE SPACES OR SMALL, THERE ARE MANY DESIGN FEATURES COMMON TO BOOKSTORES THAT WE CAN HARNESS AND REINTERPRET IN OUR OWN INTERIOR SPACES. THE LIGHTING IN MY FAVOURITE STORE, FOR EXAMPLE, IS LOW AND MOODY. THE AMBER-COLOURED LIGHT FITTINGS HANGING

INSPIRATIONAL ELEMENTS:
WISE
AMBIENT
WARM
ABSORBING
COSY
PEACEFUL

FROM THE CEILING CREATE A LOVELY, GENTLE GLOW, JUST ENOUGH LIGHT TO LET YOU SEE WHAT YOU ARE READING, BUT SUBDUED ENOUGH TO ALLOW YOU TO ESCAPE FROM THE WORLD FOR A WHILE. A COLOUR PALETTE OF GREY AND DEEP CHARCOAL ON THE WALLS AND SHELVES LENDS A SENSE OF MYSTERY TO THE SPACE, GIVING THE BROWSER THE OPPORTUNITY TO HIDE AMONG THE SHADOWS. AND OF COURSE, A QUIET CORNER TO READ IN, WITH AN OVERSIZED ARMCHAIR AND LIBRARY-LIKE BENCH SEAT AND TABLE, PROVIDES THE PERFECT EXCUSE TO LAZE FOR HOURS, ABSORBED IN A FAVOURITE NOVEL OR TWO. SO NEXT TIME YOU SPEND AN AFTERNOON IN A BOOKSTORE, HAVE A LOOK AROUND AT THE DESIGN ELEMENTS THAT MAKE UP THAT SPACE. YOU MAY FIND YOURSELF IN POSSESSION NOT JUST OF THE LATEST THRILLER, BUT OF THRILLING NEW DECORATING IDEAS AS WELL.

WHEN WE INVITE OTHERS IN TO OUR HOMES, WE BRING TOGET-HER PEOPLE WITH DIFFERENT IDEAS AND WAYS OF LIVING — AND WITH THEM, AN OPPORTUNITY TO MOULD AND RESHAPE OUR OWN VIEW OF THINGS.

entertaining spaces

FORGE CONNECTIONS WITH FRIENDS AND FAMILY

It's such a privilege to be invited into a person's home, particularly in this day and age when, as a general rule, we form our social connections and entertain ourselves beyond our own front doors. We eat in restaurants, drink in bars, hang out in cafés, party in parks and so on — so much so that inviting friends over for lunch or being invited to a dinner party has become a rare experience. But really, is there any better way to forge connections with the people you value than having them over and sharing a meal? Even if it's a simple Sunday brunch of fruit, French toast and strong coffee, entertaining family and friends can be one of the most satisfying pastimes. It's a way to bring people together and to touch base with each other's lives in a relaxed and honest setting.

Do you entertain often? If so, how do you like to entertain: in a small, more intimate setting with a few friends and a good bottle of wine, or more rowdily with cocktails, party food and loud music? A Sunday barbecue outside on the deck could be more your style. Tracking the way that you like to interact with people is the first step to pinning down just how you like to entertain. After all, entertaining is all about connection. Look to the types of restaurants, bars and pubs where you prefer to spend your time, as a guide. Do you love small, cosy settings with low lighting and laid-back grooves? Perhaps a communal table, where all sorts of people from all sorts of places are thrown together? Maybe sitting on the floor around a coffee table is more your style? Spend a moment looking at these places in an objective way and absorb the atmosphere. Which are

the places that you keep returning to? What are the elements that make up that space? Observe the layout of the furniture, the detail in the decoration — that is, the colours, textures, fabrics and so on — and the lighting. Then emulate that feeling in your home, even if it is simply a nod to a particular style rather than the complete ensemble. If you are a party person, then funky lighting, bright-coloured furniture and, of course, a bar fridge, are what you need to get you in the mood for fun. If you are a small-gathering type, then intimate table settings with comfortable chairs, candles and textured upholstery will do the trick. If you are an outdoors type, a garden designed for relaxed gatherings will suit you best.

LAYOUT

If you love to entertain, it's important to design the layout of your furniture to suit the way in which you prefer to interact with your guests. There are numerous spaces in the house that could be devoted to entertaining, depending on the nature of the gathering. The kitchen, the dining and lounge rooms, and the terrace, garden or balcony are all possibilities. Keep in mind that the premise behind entertaining is to touch base with people and so you need to ensure that your furniture allows you to do just that. Chairs, sofas and tables should all be balanced in a way that creates easy associations between your friends. There's nothing more irritating than your guests having to shout across a room to be heard. If the dining room is your choice of entertaining space, make sure that the table height is comfortable for most people. Too high and you'll feel like Goldilocks waiting for her porridge, too low and the tall ones among you will feel squished up like Alice in Wonderland down the rabbit hole. The trick is to create an environment that entices your guests to linger and enjoy the meal that you have created for them. Low lighting helps too, particularly if you are like me and cooking is not your strong point.

> '**SPACE AND LIGHT AND ORDER.**
> THOSE ARE THE THINGS MEN NEED JUST AS MUCH AS THEY NEED
> **BREAD OR A PLACE TO SLEEP.'** *LE CORBUSIER*

COLOUR

Colour affects our mood, in ways that we often don't register. And the colour of the space in which you are entertaining, combined with the food that you are serving, can have a real influence on your appetite and the general wellbeing of your guests. If you prefer a quiet, intimate setting, a palette of warm neutrals, mixed in with some earth-coloured accents, will lull your guests into a state of relaxation. If party scenes are more your thing, bright colours in acid shades and bold, geometric patterns will get the place really pumping. For a casual barbecue outside, a crisp palette of indigo blue and aqua will keep everyone feeling relaxed but perky. Throw in some bold floral patterns to remind your guests how wonderful life really can be.

DETAIL

As is always the case, the little details will really bring your entertaining spaces alive. Beautiful tableware and napery that complement the food you are serving are essential in the dining room. Mix and match vintage pieces for an individual touch. Keeping it all white is the perfect backdrop for any meal. Glassware is important at parties, particularly if cocktails are on the menu. Nothing beats a cocktail in a glass made for cocktails, so invest in a set if you're the party animal type. A series of bijou vases, placed in a line along the table centre (and filled with a single flower each) is a simple but beautiful gesture. Tea lights in clusters help to add to the ambience. However, the meal will be the real star of any gathering. Keep your menu simple to ensure that you appeal to all tastes and do as much preparation before your guests arrive as you can. Remember that a dinner with a host stuck in the kitchen is not much of a party at all. Unless, of course, your kitchen caters for many — in which case keep the party in the kitchen. There's nothing more satisfying than enlisting friends to help in the preparation of the meal; what better way is there to bring people together?

THE PERSONAL SPACES WE INHABIT SHOULD REFLECT THE EXPERIENCES OF OUR LIFE SO FAR — AND IN TURN, SUPPORT THE MEMORIES WE ARE IN THE MIDST OF CREATING.

transitional spaces

PATHWAYS LEADING THROUGH OUR HOMES

We often neglect our transitional spaces — that is, our hallways, pathways and entrance areas — focusing more on the design and decoration of the grand spaces that lie beyond them. It's probably because we tend not to dwell in these areas. They work more as a runway to better things, and so it seems much more worthwhile to concentrate our energies on the decoration of the rooms that we spend most of our time living in. But in actual fact, the way that you address your transitional spaces will have just as much impact on the experience of living in your home. Transitional spaces are 'taster' spaces if you like, an introduction to what you'll find in the rooms that lie ahead. They can set up the mood of your home by lulling you into the atmosphere or energy that you will find swirling within the walls of the rest of your house. They are the veins of a house, the connective spaces that keep the life and energy pumping into the heart-centre of your home. Transitional spaces help to keep your home alive and can tell you as much (or often more) about a person, their interests and style, as any other room in the house.

Hotels know only too well the importance of the transitional space: their foyers, check-in areas and waiting spaces set up the tone of the establishment, branding it with the flavour and ambience the owners wish to convey to their prospective clientele. In fact, the design of a foyer can advertise, better than anything else, what type of place you are stepping into and will give you a good indication of what you will find in the rooms beyond. Everything from the proportions of the space, to the flooring, lighting, upholstery, colour scheme and calibre of artwork, gives you a sense of what the hotel is trying to convey, whether it be a glamorous establishment, a funky bohemian space or a hostel. You need only take one step into the foyer to know what you're dealing with and how deep you have to dig to spend a night there.

What kind of transitional spaces connect the rooms in your house? Do you have a foyer area that announces your daily arrival and the arrival of your

'I DON'T THINK THERE IS ANYTHING WRONG WITH WHITE SPACE.

I DON'T THINK IT'S A PROBLEM

TO HAVE A BLANK WALL.' *ANNIE LEIBOVITZ*

visitors? Maybe it is one long corridor, with rooms situated either side of it. Perhaps it is a rambling garden pathway that sweeps you up into the home that lies beyond. Regardless of the type of space, it's important to design and decorate connective spaces in a way that reflects what you are trying to say in your home, that embodies the tone and the energy of the space in which you are living. An all-white entrance area, with little in the way of embellishment, advertises a no-fuss kind of space, one not concerned with the details of daily life. A bright and colourful space indicates an upbeat, happy home. A dark and moody transitional space works to lull you into the deep, cocooning energy of a dramatically decorated space. Or perhaps an element of surprise represents your living code more than anything. An overgrown garden could lead you to a bright, contemporary space beyond. Why not? It's up to you to decide the energy that best represents your approach to life.

DECORATE

It's up to the decoration of your transitional space to convey the image or energy of the rest of your home. Transitional spaces are mostly devoid of the bold architectural features that stamp your other spaces with personality, and so your use of carpeting, lighting, detail and artwork is what will really brand this space with individuality and verve. Long hall runners will create a clear pathway, leading you by the hand, so to speak, into the other rooms of your home. Choose tribal kelim rugs for a more exotic flavour; Persian rugs to convey a luscious feeling of indulgence; contemporary, geometric patterns for a modern twist; or the texture of sisal rugs if you'd like a foot rub on the way. Artwork is another important element in a transitional space. A series of paintings, fabric hangings, framed embroidered pieces or objets d'art all work to create a talking point in an otherwise vacant space. Hat racks invite your guests to dwell in the foyer before being led to the goodies that lie beyond. Only use larger items of furniture like chairs, chests and cabinets if you still have enough room to navigate through the space with ease.

alfresco spaces

CONNECTING WITH THE NATURAL WORLD

A connection to the outdoors reminds us, more than anything else, of our need for a relationship with nature. Regardless of our location, whether we live in an urban high rise or a country shack, we all need a sense of nature and the natural to maintain our physical, mental and emotional wellbeing. Even if you make the merest nod to nature — for example a single pot plant on an otherwise bare balcony — the effects of this simple gesture will resonate in the soul, and in the mind. Our outdoor spaces entice us to dream, providing a backdrop that allows and encourages relaxation and a reconnection with the spirit. Even the most hard-core urbanites among us need that connection sometimes — or at least need to know that it is there for the taking when required. In New York, apartments with rooftop gardens are the most sought-after buildings to live in; in London, townhouses that have courtyard gardens are the most coveted. In Sydney, even the highest buildings feature balconies, allowing their inhabitants to cross the threshold from indoors to outdoors and absorb the wonderful external energy — as well as observe goings-on below.

What kind of outdoor spaces do you need to fill your soul and make you feel complete? Of course, architecture dictates to some degree the size and proportion of our outdoor spaces, particularly if you are a city dweller; however, for those who need a connection to the outdoors to maintain their equilibrium, even the smallest balcony can do the trick. My mother lives in a small apartment with little in the way of an outdoor space except for a sliver of a balcony about 60 x 150 centimetres (that's 2 feet by 5 feet). Originally from the country, and possessing a passion and a talent for planting, she has filled this space to the brim with rows and rows of pots, all painted in her favourite colour palette of pink and sage green and planted with a mélange of whatever takes her fancy. You could hardly call this an outdoor space — she can barely fit a chair out there. However, the connection with the outdoors and with the flowers she loves that her garden represents is what she uses as a tool to create balance and harmony in herself and her life.

You may be fortunate enough to possess more space to dally with, in which case pinpointing what you need from your outdoor spaces and how you want them to work for you will guide the way you design and decorate them. Do you love entertaining? Is there anything more satisfying for you than bringing together groups of loved ones for a long and lazy afternoon get together? In this case a shrine to the beloved barbecue is a must for you. Or if cooking is a true passion, an outdoor kitchen could be the hub of your outdoor space. Or a pizza oven could be what you need, to feed the hungry hoards. Maybe you love to play — which means your garden should be designed in a way to encourage amusement and fun. A swimming pool, of course, will provide hours of fun and games, but even just a cleared area for playing cricket or boules could be all that you need. If the heat of the day is too much to cope with, but a connection to the outdoors is your ideal way to idle away a Sunday, a pergola draped with a passion fruit vine or a mass of bougainvillea flowers for shade could do the trick. Maybe a table and a single chair for one will encourage you to stop for a while. As is always the case, look around you for inspiration and think objectively about the spaces you find yourself in. But more importantly, connect with your instincts, with how a space makes you feel. When it comes to nature and all of its riches, think first with your heart for the clearest guidance.

03
making
spaces

TO CREATE EXCITING AND INDIVIDUAL SPACES, YOU NEED TO
IDENTIFY THE KINDS OF ENVIRONMENTS
THAT UPLIFT AND INSPIRE YOU. THEN
COMBINE THAT KNOWLEDGE WITH AN UNDERSTANDING
OF THE FUNDAMENTALS OF INTERIOR DESIGN.

So, how are you feeling now? I hope that Chapter 2 has given you some clue to the types of spaces that you love to live in — and in the process, a clearer insight into how you like, and need, to live to get the most out of life. For example, it could be that you are living in a household full of people, all leading hectic, crazy lives. By taking the time to think about the spaces that truly inspire you, you might have discovered that what you need to get through the day is a quiet, sacred space where you can completely unwind and shed your stresses. Now, of course, I'm not suggesting here that drastic changes (like moving out into a space just for one) is what you need to do, but a designated space of your own in the house could be enough to make you smile. On the other hand, you may be living alone — and have discovered that the wild chaos of communal living really fuels your fire. Perhaps it is a

mixture of both, in which case allocating different spaces for different activities is a good solution for you. In my household, it is my husband who needs some time (and space) to himself, to help him navigate through daily life, and so he has a quiet corner (we live in a small house) that is all his. The rest of us are communal people — or more to the point, wherever I go, the children (and the dog) follow — and so we seem to get by, all thrown in together, sharing each other's floor space. Whatever it is that you personally need from your space, it is important to come up with an outcome and an interior that work for everyone who lives in the home.

And so, now that you have some idea about the types of spaces that you want to create, you need the tools to make it happen. Having a connection with yourself and your loves is only part of the puzzle. To see the vision for your interior through to fruition you need an understanding of the fundamentals of interior design. On the pages that follow, I'm going to lead you through some design theory, the basics that everyone needs to use when they are planning a redesign of their spaces. It sounds rather boring, I know, particularly if you are someone who likes to skip straight to the fun stuff: that is, choosing colours, fabrics, furniture and so on. However, without the basic design knowledge at hand to help

ONCE YOU HAVE ESTABLISHED WHAT YOU NEED FROM YOUR SPACE ON AN EMOTIONAL LEVEL, YOU ARE FREE TO START EXPERIMENTING WITH THE CREATIVITY OF DESIGN AND DECORATION.

'WHO IN THE WORLD AM I?

AH, THAT IS THE GREAT PUZZLE.' *LEWIS CARROLL*

guide your choices, you could end up with a mish-mash of furniture and decoration that will, in fact, create more problems for you down the track. These two aspects must work together to complete the picture.

I like to think of the fundamentals of design as the foundation of your space: you need to have your foundation in place before you move on to the next stage. Without a solid foundation, or a strong root system, your decoration will seem trivial and flimsy; it will have nothing to underpin it and therefore nothing to prevent it from just keeling over. As with creativity of any kind, an understanding of the basics is the first step. Even so, once you have developed a strong relationship with the fundamentals, don't labour over them too much. To my mind, interiors created with some sense of self-abandonment are the most exciting homes to be a part of. So have some fun — experiment with the theory, turn it on its head to see if that creates a better result in your space. It is all a process of trial and error, in the course of which you may just find that 'the rules' don't work for you at all. Although you may feel that you need to make all of your choices before you take the first step, sometimes it's the surprises that come out of experimentation that make for the most exciting elements in a room. Take your time. Although having an all-encompassing vision for your home is important in order to create a cohesive interior, work through that vision room by room to ensure that the project doesn't overwhelm you. And just remember that we all have to start somewhere ... the key is just to begin.

the layout of space

Every space you find yourself in is unique, and so it's important to assess the space by focusing on its individual merits and deficits. The aim is to create balance – that fine line we tread between order and disorder – in our homes and in our lives.

Although it is important to think about the whole house as one space — thereby ultimately ensuring a flow of colour, pattern and form throughout — isolating every room from the next can be a simpler way to 'get your head around' the sheer scale of the project.

As an exercise in the assessment of your spaces, choose one room in your house to concentrate on: let's say it's the lounge room. Look at the size of this space, its orientation to the sun, whether or not it has a connection to the outdoors, whether or not it is protected from the wind and the weather. Is it a small or a large space?

What are the activities that you are planning on performing there? Will the space accommodate those needs? Are you already squeezing your life into an overcrowded lounge room? Your choice of furniture and decoration, then, should reflect your answers to these questions. Do you feel like you are a small fish swimming around in an oversized living area? Larger items of furniture combined with smaller vignettes of decoration will help to fill up the space. Take a look at the wall space — is the room broken up by windows? Are you dealing with complete walls or slivers of wall that flow from one room to the next? Does the architecture, or the framework, of the room look busy to your eye? If so, simplifying that busyness with modern, clean-lined furniture could create a sense of spaciousness.

SIT BACK AND TAKE A LOOK AT HOW THE SPACE WORKS WITHIN THE IMPRINT OF YOUR HOME. HAVING ESTABLISHED ITS ARCHITECTURE, YOU CAN BEGIN TO MANIPULATE THE AMBIENCE WITHIN THE SPACE.

A SIMPLE PALETTE OF WHITE, PUNCTUATED WITH AN ELEMENT OF WHIMSY IN THE DECORATION, CREATES A FEELING OF EXPANSIVENESS AND A SENSE OF FLOW IN WHAT IS A VERY SMALL KITCHEN.

Once you have assessed your space just by using your naked eye, take a pencil and a piece of paper and draw the room. You don't need a degree in architecture for this, just a simple sketch will do. Mark in where the windows and the doors are situated and any other fixed elements such as bookshelves and storage areas. Now use some coloured pencils to draw your furniture and all of the other bits and bobs that fill that space. How is it looking to your eye? Busy? Sparse, perhaps? Are the items of furniture arranged in a way to promote flow and ease of activity? Is the sofa taking advantage of the afternoon sunshine? Does the drawing appear to be balanced, the scale of each piece of furniture happily cohabiting with the scale of the other? Once you have completed your drawing, leave it for a while and attend to other things. Then, come back to it again. How does it look now? It's important when designing anything to give yourself some time to reflect on the task at hand. Time is one of the greatest assets you have in ensuring that the development of your space ultimately suits your needs. So, take the time — in doing so you will allow your senses a moment to get a good handle on what you are trying to achieve.

Once you have returned to your original sketch, and digested its form, draw the layout of the room again, leaving out the furniture and decoration detail. This time, look at your drawing in isolation from the room it depicts (and from all of its bits and bobs), then fill it with your ideal layout scenario. Use your instinct to create a sense of balance in the space, assessing how the arrangement of your furniture on the page makes you feel at first glance. In an ideal world, the room and all of its elements would be balanced, designed with a sense of symmetry and order. However, in reality, our rooms come in all shapes and sizes — squares, rectangles, L-shapes and so on — and it is important that you look to your particular layout and take in all of its foibles. Understanding the layout of the space that you are dealing with is the first step. Once you have grasped this, it's time to work out some solutions.

odd spaces

Addressing a space that is out of the ordinary, that is an odd shape with a less-than-ideal orientation, can be one of the most daunting aspects of interior design.

It is often easier to do nothing at all than it is to begin the process of addressing the numerous design issues these spaces throw up. However, all spaces, regardless of their design fundamentals, can be reworked and improved with a little attention and remoulding. Never give up on any space just because it isn't packaged perfectly, as sometimes these spaces end up being the most exciting ones to spend your time in.

For rooms with little light, use a light and airy colour scheme to maximize and reflect the light that you do have. Spaces with too much light need to be toned down. Do this with more subdued colour schemes that will absorb the light, in addition to using good-quality blockout shutters, blinds and backed curtains on the windows so that you have control over the abundance of light. Of course, you could turn this advice on its head if you love the dark and dramatic ambience of a boudoir, and fill your low-lit room with deep, moody colours and oversized furniture. If you want to maximize the light in an already glary room, decorate with the light-reflective palette of white and all of its tones. Remember, though, that this is all about creating individuality — so you may wish to disregard 'the rules' to suit yourself.

Large, warehouse-style spaces should be filled with a series of smaller furniture vignettes to enclose the space, making it feel cosier and more comfortable. Use a clash of warm colours and patterns to achieve this effect. And of course, a display of over-sized rugs — I prefer kelims and tribal rugs, in this instance, as their patterns and weaves will create interest from the floor up.

MAKING A FEATURE OF AN OTHERWISE ODD SPACE ADDS AN ELEMENT OF ECCENTRICITY TO THIS WAREHOUSE BEDROOM.

SIMPLE GESTURES, SUCH AS THIS OPEN SHELVING UNIT, HELP TO
CREATE UNIFICATION BETWEEN THE KITCHEN AND LIVING SPACES.

'CREATIVITY IS A TYPE OF LEARNING PROCESS
WHERE THE TEACHER AND PUPIL ARE LOCATED
IN THE SAME INDIVIDUAL.' *ARTHUR KOESTLER*

In small spaces, you need to create the illusion of having more space by tricking the eye with simple lines and sparse decoration. Go for contemporary designs with little in the way of embellishment to give your small space room to breathe. Put clutter behind built-in cupboards and choose multi-purpose furniture where you can, to cut down on the number of items that you need to fill the space. A soft, pale palette will add to the illusion; stick with bold, geometric patterns (stripes and Marimekko styles) to limit the busyness.

Then, of course, you've got those weird and wonderful spaces that come in a shape that has no rhyme or reason. I consider L-shaped rooms to be a part of this pack, as are those funny little alcoves that sit off a main room but seem to have no purpose of their own. What does one do with these mix and match spaces? Remember that the aim is to create balance even when the framework of the room has little to suggest it. Colour is a great tool here — a strong colour that extends from the lounge room (or bedroom) to that little alcove that I just mentioned would create the illusion that it is part of the larger space. Apply the same principle to the L-shape. Another tool is to designate one end of the L-shape for a different activity, to give it a sense of distinction. This would be a possibility for a combined lounge and dining room. An L-shaped bedroom could be used as a sleeping area and an office area, divided by the natural partition that the L-shape provides. Your choice of lighting can also help: in this instance, soft, ambient light for the sleeping section and stronger, more prominent light for your working space will promote the illusion of a larger space. Play around with your options — again, the process of trial and error will get you to where you need to be.

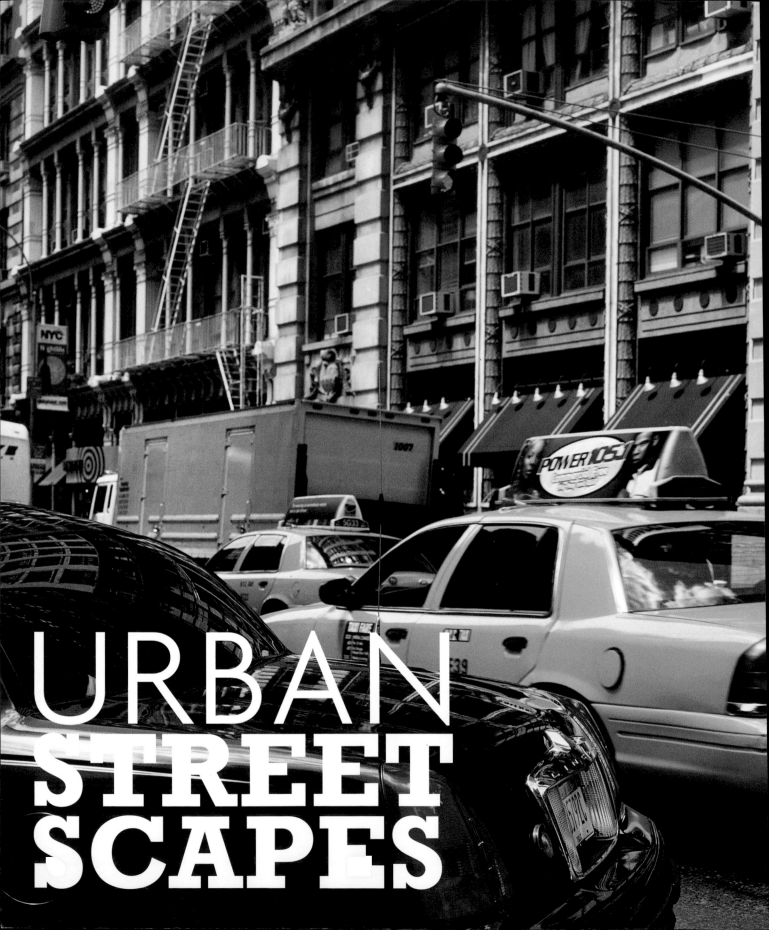

URBAN
STREET
SCAPES

OUR CITIES ARE FRENETIC SPACES — A HIVE OF COLOUR, TEXTURE AND PATTERN. DRAW UPON THIS HARD-EDGED PALETTE FOR YOUR OWN HOME IF YOU ENJOY RAW ENERGY AND THE FEELING OF THE BLOOD PUMPING THROUGH YOUR VEINS.

DON'T YOU JUST LOVE THE BUZZ OF THE CITY: THE SOUND OF SIRENS, THE SYMPHONY OF CAR HORNS, PEOPLE'S FOOTSTEPS, CHILDREN LAUGHING, TRAMS OR BUSES CLAMOURING AND SUBWAYS ROARING — ALL SET AMID A LANDSCAPE OF HIGH RISE BUILDINGS AND CONCRETE FOOTPATHS? THERE IS SOMETHING SIMULTANEOUSLY INVIGORATING AND EXHAUSTING ABOUT SPENDING TIME IN AN URBAN LANDSCAPE. IT BRINGS SENSORY OVERLOAD, WITH YOUR SENSES OF SIGHT, SOUND, TOUCH, TASTE AND SMELL ALL WORKING OVERTIME TO COPE WITH THE INTENSE, UNRELENTING PACE OF THE INNER CITY. CITIES ARE LOUD AND BOISTEROUS PLACES WHICH NEVER SLEEP, WHICH ARE IN CONSTANT MOTION. THE ENERGY THAT RISES FROM THE VERY CRACKS IN THE SIDEWALKS IS EXCITING AND UPLIFTING — IT KEEPS ALL THOSE WHO HURRY ALONG THE CITY STREETS ON THE ALERT, HYPER-AWARE.

TO MY MIND, NEW YORK IS PROBABLY THE BEST EXAMPLE OF ALL THAT A CITY COULD BE. IT IS AN INTENSE PLACE; SO MUCH EMOTION REVERBERATES WITHIN IT, SO MUCH EXPECTATION AND SO MUCH HOPE. OLD BLUE EYES SINGS 'IF I CAN MAKE IT THERE, I'LL MAKE IT ANYWHERE', AND THIS SENTIMENT IS SHARED BY ALL WHO ARE PREPARED TO TAKE ON ITS MIGHT. TIME SPENT VISITING NEW YORK ALWAYS LEAVES ME ENERGIZED — EVEN AFTER SPENDING JUST A FEW DAYS THERE I COME AWAY WITH MY HEAD FULL OF IDEAS AND MY HEART FULL OF GREAT MEMORIES. MANY FACTORS GIVE THIS CITY ITS UNIQUE EDGE AND EXHILARATING VIBE: THE HIGH RISE BLOCKS SET AGAINST THE TRANQUILLITY OF CENTRAL PARK, THE COBBLED STREETS OF THE DOWNTOWN DISTRICT, THE FLASHING YELLOW OF THE TAXI CABS AND THE ENERGY EMANATING FROM MILLIONS OF PEOPLE VYING FOR SPACE ON AN ISLAND WHERE SPACE IS CONSIDERED GOLD.

THINK ABOUT ALL THE URBAN CENTRES YOU HAVE VISITED. WHAT ARE THE ELEMENTS THAT MAKE SOME CITIES SUCH A THRILLING PLACE TO BE? WHAT IS THE OVERRIDING MOOD OF THE CITY YOU LOVE THE MOST? JUST LIKE A HOME, EACH CITY DRAWS ITS UNIQUE SENSE OF STYLE FROM ITS LAYOUT AND FORM, COUPLED WITH THE AMBIENCE OF THE LIFE TAKING PLACE WITHIN IT ON THE STREETS, AND IN THE OFFICES, SHOPS AND HOMES.

WHAT DOES YOUR FAVOURITE CITY LOOK LIKE? IS IT CRAMMED TO THE BRIM

INSPIRATIONAL ELEMENTS:
RAW
INDUSTRIAL
RELENTLESS
CHAOTIC

WITH BUILDINGS, NEON LIGHTS AND CHAOS LIKE NEW YORK, OR IS IT A CALM PLACE WHERE ADEQUATE SPACE ALLOWS THE LIGHT TO SHINE ONTO THE STREETS THROUGHOUT THE DAY, AS IN COPENHAGEN? PERHAPS BARCELONA SPEAKS TO YOU MOST DIRECTLY, THIS CITY WHERE THE COLOURFUL, HIGHLY DECORATED, BUILDINGS OF GAUDI, FRAMED AGAINST A BACKDROP OF MOUNTAINS AND BLUE SEA, PUNCTUATE THE GREY GRUNGE OF THE TINY LANEWAYS.

SPEND TIME REMEMBERING THE CITIES YOU HAVE REACTED TO MOST STRONGLY. LEAF THROUGH YOUR PHOTO ALBUMS AND TAKE NOTE OF THE PICTURES THAT MOST INSPIRE YOU. HAVE A LOOK AT THE DETAIL OF THE PLACE, THE LITTLE BITS AND PIECES THAT MAKE UP THE LIFE THERE. IN THE CASE OF NEW YORK, IS THIS FRENETIC FEELING SOMETHING THAT YOU WOULD LIKE TO TRANSLATE INTO YOUR OWN HOME?

AS I MENTIONED EARLIER, HOW YOU MANOEUVRE THE ELEMENTS OF DESIGN — HOW YOU USE COLOUR, FORM, LIGHT, LAYOUT AND SO ON TO CONCOCT YOUR RECIPE FOR LIVING — CAN HAVE A HUGE IMPACT ON THE AMBIENCE OF THE SPACE YOU'RE IN. SO, IF A LITTLE BIT OF CHAOS IS WHAT FUELS YOUR FIRE, YOUR FAVOURITE CITY COULD BE JUST THE PLACE THAT YOU TURN TO FOR SOME DESIGN INSPIRATION.

placing furniture

There's nothing that I loved more as a child than role-playing my fantasy life using Barbie and her friends as the stars.

It began with one lonely Barbie at the age of about eight years old; however, the family soon grew to include Ken, Skipper, GI Joe and an extra Barbie or two in varying incarnations — ballet Barbie, beach Barbie and so on. What really got the party going for me was the inclusion of Barbie furniture in my Christmas stocking. After all, what can you do with Barbie unless she has a setting within which she can exist? Perhaps, for me, it was a sign of things to come, that the environment or the spaces that Barbie was to move through became just as important to me as the dolls themselves. It was the spaces that I created that gave my games a sense of meaning. Without the furniture, Barbie was just a neglected toy that I left to hang out under the dining room table.

What on earth does all of this have to do with the decoration of your interior? Well, it's important when trying to come to grips with the layout and scale of your space to have an understanding of how the furniture that you use to fill up a room balances with the framework of the space itself. It is often difficult to grasp this concept with the naked eye; most of us need a solid and a more tangible plan to work with. As I mentioned earlier, drawing a floor plan is one way to understand how the scale of your room works with the scale of the furniture that you plan to put in it. Sketch the room on paper, then draw your items of furniture to scale on a separate sheet. Colour them in and then cut them out. Place them on the floor plan in groupings that create balance and harmony, to get some sense of how to resolve your aims.

The other way is to pull out all of the old Barbie or Ken stuff that you had when you were a child — beds, sofas, chairs and lamps — and begin to place them in configurations that mimic your real life items. Move them around until you are satisfied with the results. Again, take your time; leave your creations for a while and return to them later with a fresh mind and viewpoint. It sounds so childlike, but it really is a wonderful way to construct a substantial model of the space that you are dealing with. And of course, it's just fun. Who said that interior design always needed an earnest approach?

FURNITURE PROVIDES THE FOUNDATION OF A SPACE. THE SUPPORT LAYER FOR THE PERSONAL TOUCHES THAT GIVE A SPACE ITS CHARACTER.

directing light

When we are assessing the decorating success of our interior spaces we rarely offer lighting much praise; we tend to pay much more attention to the detail of colour, form and patterning.

But in actuality, lighting plays a crucial role in the overall finished effect of your space. Lighting influences us in subtle ways; the impact is subliminal rather than conscious, so much so that we tend only to notice its negative effects when we are subjected to the rotten kind of lighting — that harsh, fluorescent light that simultaneously prematurely ages our facial features and induces the onset of a headache.

However, it's important to consider your lighting preferences seriously when you are making your decorating choices. Think about how important the role of lighting is when you are next at the theatre watching a play or operatic performance. Designers can create beautiful costuming and stage sets, but without the support of the lighting it's impossible to get a true sense of the story. In the same way, paying heed to how lighting is working in your home will have a great influence on the way that you are living within it.

And so, have a look at your space — at all times of the day or night. Does it receive direct sunshine? If so, at what time of the day? Does it wake you up in the morning when you are lying in bed or greet you in the lounge room at afternoon teatime? Perhaps your space lacks direct sunlight completely: tall buildings or large trees might overshadow it. Monitor how the light works over time — and over the seasons — as it can be a moveable feast. Once you have tracked your natural light patterns, think about how that lighting makes you feel, what kind of mood the light creates in your space and the effect that this is having on you. Your decorating response will be greatly influenced by this mood. If a lack of natural light leaves you feeling depressed, your aim will be to maximize light through the use of colour

126127

[SENSEOFSTYLESPACE] COLOUR, TEXTURE, FORM, LIGHT AND LAYOUT — EMPLOY ALL OF THE ELEMENTS OF DESIGN TO CREATE A UNIFIED SPACE

and furniture placement. Pale colours, which reflect the already available light, and furniture placed away from windows and light sources, are good solutions for you. If your space has too much light and you want to minimize the glare, choose deeper tones that absorb the light and fill your space with larger items of furniture to make your space cosier. Plantation shutters, backed blinds or curtains on the windows are a good option also, allowing you more control over the amount of light that you are receiving throughout the day. Of course, you may love your dark and moody boudoir — the womb-like space may make you feel supported and nurtured. In this case, fill up a dark room with dark furniture to maximize the effect. This is a book about developing individuality and a unique sense of style, after all, and so it is important that your reaction to light reflects your own feeling for it. Maybe lots of glary light is your thing: if so, go for light colours — white is the best — that work to bounce the light all around the room. A warning though: you may need a good, strong pair of sunglasses to keep the frown lines at bay.

'IT'S A HELLUVA START, BEING ABLE
TO RECOGNIZE WHAT MAKES YOU HAPPY.'
LUCILLE BALL

Once you have a good idea of how the natural light is working in your space, it's time to think about how to use artificial light to fill in the gaps. Not all artificial lighting is created equal, however, so think about the solution that best addresses your concerns. As I mentioned before, fluorescent lighting will emit a harsh, glary light and give even the most comfortable spaces dental-lab-like overtones. So steer clear of it wherever possible. Recessed halogen downlights are a more sympathetic option as they illuminate with a gentler, more natural type of light, and their dimming ability will mean that you have more control of the type of light that you are receiving. You will find that lamp lighting offers you the moodiest, most evocative type of light. Lamp lighting is generally low lighting — unless you need it for reading, in which case go for a bright, office-like option — and as such will create a soft, gentle environment for you to relax in. The wonder of lamp lighting is that it is portable and can be mixed and matched to suit your decoration and your situation. If you feel like you are swimming in a large, warehouse-style space, choose a series of floor lamps to create smaller vignettes and cosy nooks. Turn on table lamps, with low wattage globes, for an intimate dinner just for two. And don't forget the benefit of candle lighting. It is the most effective tool to use at the end of a busy day when you want to block out the mess around you and just settle in for the evening.

EATERIES

WHAT BETTER INSPIRATION IS THERE WHEN DECORATING AN EATING SPACE THAN YOUR FAVOURITE RESTAURANT? LOOK AT THE ELEMENTS THAT MAKE UP THE SPACE AND HOW THEY WORK TOGETHER TO CREATE AMBIENCE.

WE ARE
SO FORTUNATE THESE DAYS TO HAVE A MULTITUDE OF WONDERFUL GASTRONOMIC DELIGHTS AT OUR FINGERTIPS. GONE ARE THE DAYS WHEN A PLATE OF OVERCOOKED MEAT AND SOGGY VEG WAS SERVED UP AS THE STANDARD EVENING REPERTOIRE. NOW, ENTIRE MENUS OF EXOTIC FLAVOURS AND ENTICING AROMAS ARE AVAILABLE IN THE TIME THAT IT TAKES TO WALK TO YOUR FAVOURITE EATERY. FOOD HAS BECOME MORE EXCITING THAN SEX, AND CHEFS SEXIER THAN ROCK STARS — AND WITH THIS HAS COME THE OPPORTUNITY FOR US ALL TO INDULGE IN ANY MANNER OF WONDROUS CULINARY CREATIONS.

BUT THE GASTRONOMIC REVOLUTION IS NOT MERELY ABOUT THE TASTE OF FOOD; IT'S ALSO ABOUT SAVOURING THE EXPERIENCE OF EATING, WHERE THE ENVIRONMENT AND AMBIENCE OF THE SPACE IN WHICH YOU ARE DINING GO HAND IN HAND WITH WHAT IS BEING SERVED ON THE MENU. WITH ALL OF THIS GREAT FARE OFTEN COMES INSPIRING INTERIOR DESIGN. NO LONGER DOES THE LOCAL FISH AND CHIPPERY LOOK LIKE A GREASED-UP DENTAL SURGERY. THESE DAYS, EATERIES FROM THE MILK BAR ON THE CORNER TO THE LOCAL PUB ARE EMPLOYING DESIGN IDEAS TO MAKE THE EXPERIENCE OF EATING (AND DRINKING) THAT MUCH SWEETER.

WHEN SOURCING INSPIRATION FOR YOUR OWN PERSONAL SPACE, WHAT BETTER WAY IS THERE THAN TO SPEND TIME DEVOURING A MEAL AT YOUR FAVOURITE RESTAURANT, OR MEETING FRIENDS FOR A DRINK AT YOUR LOCAL BAR? TAKE THE TIME TO ABSORB NOT JUST THE FOOD AND DRINK, BUT ALSO THE ATMOSPHERE THAT IS BEING DRUMMED UP WITHIN THE SPACE AND BY THE LAYOUT OF THE SPACE. WHAT EFFECT IS THE COLOUR SCHEME HAVING ON THE WAY THAT YOU FEEL WHEN YOU SPEND A LENGTH OF TIME SURROUNDED BY IT? WHAT ABOUT THE TEXTURES: IS THE ROOM FILLED WITH A CALMING PALETTE OF BLONDE WOOD AND NEUTRAL FABRICS OR DOES IT AROUSE THE SENSES WITH COLLIDING

INSPIRATIONAL ELEMENTS:
LIVELY AROMATIC HEART-WARMING SATISFYING JOYOUS

FORM, PATTERNS AND WILD COLOURS? WHAT EFFECT DOES THE ORIENTATION OF THE SPACE HAVE ON YOU? DO YOU FIND THE WARMTH OF THE DIRECT SUNLIGHT UPLIFTING? DOES THE MOODINESS OF LOW LIGHTING MAKE YOU FEEL COCOONED AND SECURE? MAYBE YOU ARE EATING ALFRESCO — IF SO, DOES THE LAYOUT OF THE LANDSCAPING WORK FOR YOU?

NOTICING HOW A ROOM IS STRUCTURED, AND REGISTERING YOUR EMOTIONAL AND INTELLECTUAL RESPONSE TO THAT STRUCTURE, WILL GIVE YOU SOME INSIGHT INTO WHAT KINDS OF ENVIRONMENTS WORK FOR YOU ... OR NOT. AS ALWAYS, IT'S IMPORTANT TO DO YOUR RESEARCH, AND SO IT'S AT THIS POINT THAT I RECOMMEND A NIGHT OR TWO (OR THREE) TRYING OUT WHAT'S ON OFFER. YOU NEVER KNOW WHAT YOU MAY DISCOVER. JUST REMEMBER, THOUGH, TO TAKE NOTES EARLY ON — ONE TOO MANY COCKTAILS AND THE SPACE COULD START SPINNING.

colour schemes

Colour is one of the most exciting tools that you can use when designing your interior spaces, as it can have more influence on the way you live and breathe in your home than anything else.

The use of colour in our homes has a two-fold effect. On a basic level, colour can help to create or add to the foundation of your room, through the use of wall and floor colours. Your choice of colours can ground your space, giving you a solid base on which to create. However, colour can also be the tool that you employ the most often when addressing the decoration and the detail of your space. If you have read *Sense of Style: Colour*, you'll have a good insight into just how much fun you can have playing with colour and all of the options it offers. But colour can be a daunting subject as well, and pinpointing an exact colour scheme to suit your lifestyle can be a lengthy process. Even so, its wonder is worth tackling, and once you have mastered negotiating the options the results can change the way you live and feel in your home.

COLOUR AS THE BACKDROP

The way that you tackle colour as the backdrop of your room will be completely different from your approach to colour in the detail and the decoration. In this instance, it's important to think about colour in the same terms you would apply to all other aspects of the framework or the architecture of your space. A backdrop colour — that is, the palette that you choose for your walls, floors, cupboards and any other fixtures — will work as the blank canvas in your room. It will be the background for all other aspects of decoration, its role being to support the layers and the detail that will be overlaid upon it. As colouring your space is often a costly project, it's important to apply a sense of good judgment to this process. Although I'm all for experimenting and having a good time with the various possibilities, it's important that you get this aspect of your room right before you move on to the other elements. Painting your space a hot shade of pink could be just what your heart desires; however, will that shade blend well with the other items with which you plan on

134135

[SENSE**OFSTYLE**SPACE] THE EVERYDAY COLOUR THAT SURROUNDS US AS WE MOVE THROUGH OUR LIVES, PROVIDES US WITH A PALETTE WE CAN DRAW UPON WHEN DECORATING OUR HOME.

filling the space? Will your choice of wall colour force you to reinvest in a brand new range of furniture? Of course, this is fine if your bank balance can cope with the strain, but if you are sticking to a budget, perhaps a more subdued tone that works with the rest of your furnishings is your best choice. It's up to you — once you have assessed your options you may find that hot pink is just what you need and you will decide to go for it anyway. Remember, colour is all about fuelling your spirit, and so a little self-abandonment could be worth it.

Use your newfound knowledge about layout and balance when making your choices. If your space is too dark, choose a light shade for the walls (and even the floors) that will help to promote a sense of space. A deeper tone, on the other hand, will create the illusion of a cosier, more cocooning environment.

Remember that paint is not the only option available to you. Research the other possibilities of wallpapering, tilework and stencilling, as these exciting tools can also infuse individuality and excitement in your space. Approach wallpapering with restraint, unless you are all for wrapping yourself in the stuff. Choose one wall as your backdrop (preferably behind a bed or a sofa) and always choose a complete wall, not one that has been broken up by windows and splintered design — otherwise the balance of your room will be affected. Wall tiles are another way to add some life to an otherwise dull space. A line of eccentrically coloured and patterned tiles around the splashbacks in your kitchen could be all that the space needs to stamp it with an air of individuality. And of course, colour in the tilework in your wet areas — bathrooms, toilet rooms and laundries — is the most effective tool to use when aiming to create a specific brand of ambience in what are otherwise fairly cold spaces.

COLOUR AS THE DETAIL

Now this is where the decorating party really gets started. It is by using colour, through the detail and decoration of your room, that we can have the most fun. Our choices of upholstery fabrics, rugs, cushions, lamp shades, curtaining and the like, are the elements that will give your room a strong sense of its own personality. And it is the colour of these different elements that will define that individuality the most. I know that for some people this aspect of interior design can be the most daunting: the choices are boundless and it is here that the process of decoration can come to a complete halt, just because of the sheer enormity of the decision-making process.

'WHEN THE HEART SPEAKS, TAKE GOOD NOTES.' *JUDITH CAMPBELL*

Think about your colour scheme as a three-part process. Begin by choosing a base colour to work with. Generally, this will be a stronger tone, again, to create a sense of foundation through your details. Upholster your larger items (like sofas) in this base colour, as the combination of the larger scale of the furniture and the stronger tones will work to build the sense of a solid framework into your space. Once you have this colour in place, choose a partner for it, a colour with which it can happily cohabit — one that balances the strength of the first tone to some degree, but which also contrasts with it to create a sense of excitement in the space. On the one hand, tonal rooms are lovely because they don't disrupt the status quo or the flow of your space. However, they also negate the aspect of subversiveness and playfulness that makes decorating so much fun and that ultimately really gives your space some oomph. Your third choice of colour should be approached with a sense of frivolity in mind — this colour is the icing on the cake, the sugar that ultimately works to bring a smile to your face.

Look for patterns that employ this colour scheme if you want to layer your palette with some movement. Toss in another colour if you dare, to throw the scheme 'off' slightly and create some added interest for the eye.

patterning

The patterns that you employ in your upholstery lend a sense of artistry to your space. They are, after all, artworks in their own right.

If you think about it, behind every pattern there is a designer who has spent days, weeks and possibly months devising, illustrating and colouring their fabrics in ways that deliver their individual 'voice'. As with artwork, fabric embodies a message that is conveyed to the observer through the choice of subject matter, colours and style — it is a dialogue that embodies a specific ethos or vision for living. It is important to think about the implications of the patterns that you choose when you are trying to whittle down your options, as the patterns can have the most distinctive voice in your room. In what period did your pattern originate? If it is a contemporary pattern, it will convey a fashionable mood and your interior will appear up to the minute because of it. Maybe you prefer tribal patterns — in which case, it's important to know which tribe created that pattern, and why. I recently came across a tribal rug that I fell in love with because of its beautiful pairing of colours and geometric patterning. The rug would be a perfect partner for my lounge room sofa; however, the price tag of any rug makes you stop and ponder the decision for a while before diving in to make the purchase. After chatting to the rug dealer, a man possessing true passion for his chosen field of interest, I learnt that this particular rug was made by a rather 'eccentric' Nepalese tribe, a laid-back, go-with-the-flow bunch whose quirky attitudes are reflected very strongly in the patterning of the rug ... which, although geometric, was not in perfect alignment or symmetry. My newfound insight is what ultimately made the sale because it embodied my infatuation with slightly offbeat things. Although the colours of any pattern may suit the decoration of your space, if the

138139

[SENSE**OF**STYLE**SPACE**] CHOOSE YOUR PATTERNING AS YOU WOULD A PAINTING. STRIKE AN EMOTIONAL CONNECTION WITH IT FIRST. AND THEN THINK ABOUT BLENDING IT INTO THE REST OF YOUR DÉCOR.

meaning behind that pattern doesn't fit with your vision for living then chances are you won't feel comfortable living with it. An understanding of the individual characteristics of the pattern and the creators behind it will ultimately give that pattern a sense of meaning and relevance to your life. So use your patterning to deliver an honest message about yourself and the life that you have chosen. You may be a modern type of person, a forward thinker, someone who lives for the here and now and relishes the 'newness' of the world. If so, then a French toile, illustrated with period French street scenes, may not be conveying the message that best reflects you. You may currently be living with wide stripes in bold colours, whereas it is the intricacy of floral details that really represents an honest reflection of yourself.

Once you have unveiled the type of pattern that you love, return to your knowledge of colour pairing to help you integrate that pattern into your interior. If you stick to this two-step process, you should find it easier to navigate the many choices that are available to you.

WHERE TO USE PATTERN

Once you have come to terms with the types of patterns that best suit your sense of style, the big question is, where should they go? The most important thing to remember when patterning your interior is to adhere to the rules of balance that I have been talking about. Not enough patterns in a room make for an overly simplistic, sparse-looking interior. However, too much pattern, in colliding colours and form, will give you a mighty big headache. Balance is the key. As a basic guide, look to dividing your patterns up in two ways: pattern as the base in your room and pattern as the detail. And never the twain shall meet! If you choose to dedicate the base palette in your room to patterning, make sure that the detail, the overriding layer, is left in simple block colours. That is, if your larger items of furniture — sofa, armchair, rug and so on — are patterned, leave the cushioning, throw rugs and curtains

'TO ME STYLE IS JUST THE OUTSIDE OF CONTENT,
AND CONTENT THE INSIDE OF STYLE,
LIKE THE OUTSIDE AND THE INSIDE OF THE HUMAN BODY.
BOTH GO TOGETHER, THEY CAN'T BE SEPARATED.'

JEAN-LUC GODARD

a solid colour. On the other hand, if you choose to keep your base items of furniture in a solid colour palette, employ patterning in your details — that is, your cushions, throws and curtaining. Now of course, you can play around the edges here and throw in a surprise pattern or two to keep you on your toes. But if you do, you should employ the base/detail rule to these pattern choices as well. If you choose an overly detailed or busy pattern, pair it with a cleaner, more geometric base pattern to allow your decoration a little room to breathe. Detailed pattern, combined with an alternating detailed pattern, makes for one very busy space. As is always my advice, it is a good idea to take your time. Snip swatches of fabric from the rolls at the fabric store, bring them home and live with them for a while. You may discover after a week or two that the love affair that you thought you were having was really just a passing interest. Or, your love may grow more and more; in which case, you know that it's time to move in together. Whatever happens though, be comforted by the fact that you can experiment and mix and match your patterns, and make your mistakes, without going to too much expense. So have a go, and build up your patterning in your own time. It will make for a very interesting interior space indeed.

PATTERN IS A MEANS OF EXPRESSING OUR CREATIVE LIFE THROUGH OUR HOMES.

texture

We humans are a tactile bunch — the way that something feels to the touch will have a great influence on our response to it.

You may cover your sofa, for example, in the most beautifully coloured, expensively priced upholstery fabric, but if it is not comfortable to sit on — or laze on, more to the point — that item of furniture will be rendered useless. It is how things feel to our touch, the texture of things, combined with all of our other sensory reactions, that ensures the success of the pieces we invest in. Think about all the textures you are interacting with on a daily basis, everything from your sofa fabric, to your bed linen and your dinnerware. What do these things feel like when you caress them, what sort of reaction do you have when you touch them? Are you lulled into a state of pure relaxation, or do your nerves jangle, making you feel on edge and irritated? As with all aspects of decoration, it's important to track your individual sensory response to texture to ensure that your choices are sitting well with your version of living.

FABRIC

As a general rule, stick with natural fibres when making your upholstery choices. Not only do they 'breathe' much better than synthetics, allowing for air flow, but they also reconnect us, if only subliminally, with the natural world around us, with the earth that literally and metaphorically grounds us.

I believe this premise should also apply when you are choosing your bed linen. Generally we are more intimate with our bed linen that with any other fibre: we spend an average of eight hours a night lying on it. Choose linen, silk or cotton to provide a sense of

144145

[SENSE**OFSTYLE**SPACE] THE THINGS THAT WE PUT OUT ON DISPLAY, THE OBJECTS THAT LINE EACH WALL, GIVE

THE STRONGEST INDICATION OF WHO WE ARE, OUR AMBITIONS AND ACHIEVEMENTS.

natural connection. Avoid polyester wherever possible — after all, is there anything scratchier and more annoying than lying on polyester sheeting, particularly if you reside in a warm climate where you are no doubt sweaty enough already? I recommend using natural fibres for everything from your bathroom towelling to your tea towels and oven mitts. Modern technology has afforded us many practical inventions that make life easier to navigate on the one hand, but negate our sensory needs on the other. Once you begin to rekindle that sensory relationship, you will never look back.

EMBELLISHMENTS

Use your sense of touch when making your choices beyond fabric — that is, every other detail in your home from your dinnerware and cutlery to vases and table cloths — as their texture will ultimately affect your enjoyment of them. Pick up the item that you intend to buy, caress it, roll it through your fingers, put it up to your face. How does it feel to you? Your first reaction will generally be your most honest one. If the piece doesn't tick all of your sensory boxes, don't invest in it — it will only irritate you over time and ultimately will be left to reside in the dark recesses of a cupboard. If you can't get to the piece because it is wrapped in plastic, as is often the case with bed linen, ask the shop assistant to open it for you so that you can touch it for yourself. Again, take your time. If you are not completely satisfied with how you feel with the piece, leave it on the shelf for someone else who has different desires and sensory reactions.

One of the main considerations when developing an individual sense of style is to ensure that all the items that make it past your front door fulfil not just a practical need but also a sensual one. The result is that you will feel more comfortable in your space and better able to enjoy an honest sense of it. At the end of the day, it will make you happier, and that's exactly what home should be doing for you.

THE ARCHITECTURE OF YOUR SPACE SHOULD GUIDE THE DECORATION OF IT, TO SOME DEGREE. LARGE, OPEN SPACES SHOULD BE FILLED WITH A MELANGE OF COLOUR AND TEXTURE TO GIVE A SENSE OF HOMELINESS AND COMFORT.

ARCHITECTURAL ELEMENTS

Consider the effect of texture when making the grander decorating gestures in your home, through use of architectural elements such as paint and wallpapering, flooring and benchtops. There are some wonderful paint options on the market these days that combine colour with texture and practicality, which can be applied to everything from the walls to the woodwork and the floors. Lime washes and 'render' effect paints (which possess a sand-like texture) are a couple of options that give the walls interest and depth. Metallic paints offer a smooth shiny effect that has the added benefit of bouncing light around a dark room, particularly if you choose a lighter tone. Flocked and metallic wallpapers afford walls a luxurious feel — you can combine them with a bold pattern to make an impressive statement.

Stonework, wood flooring and carpeting all affect how we live in our spaces. If the material that you employ underfoot doesn't sit well with your nervous system, you will never feel quite right in your space. If rough stonework produces the same feeling in you as someone running their fingernails down a chalkboard, steer clear of this option and choose a smooth, glazed finish instead. On the other hand, recycled floorboards may evoke in you a strong recollection of and connection with the countryside where you spent your childhood, in which case this option, rather than floorboards with a polyurethane coating, will suit your needs. The best way to get a sense of it, of course, is to take your shoes off and walk across each option when you're at the showroom. These are big decisions to make, and so it's important that you are comfortable with them.

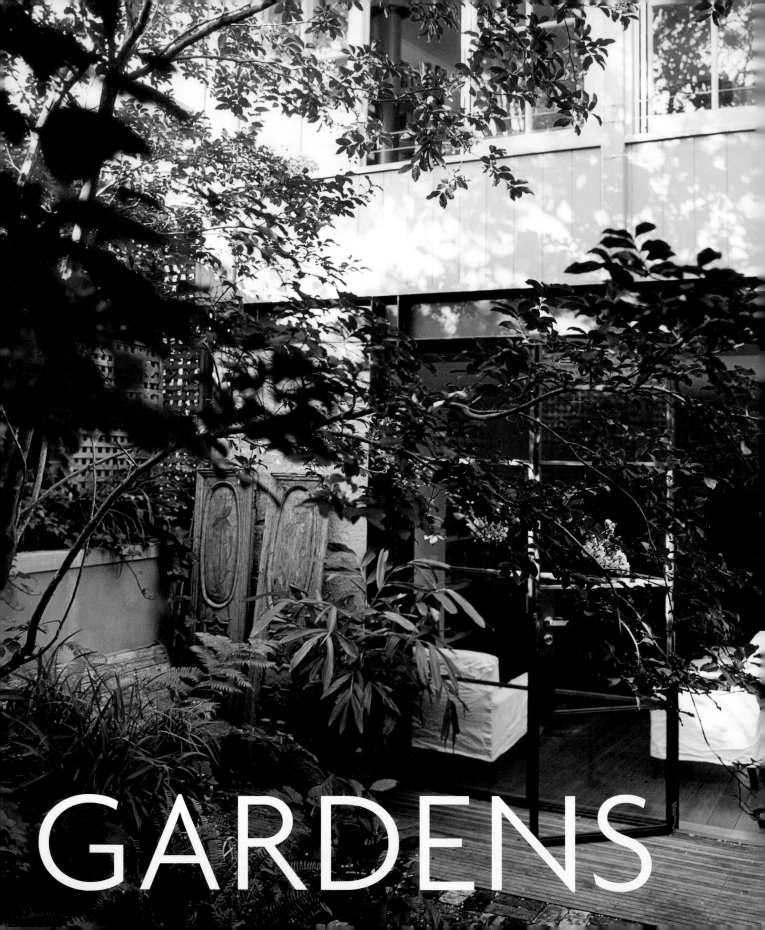

GARDENS

NO MATTER HOW LIMITED AND HUMBLE, WE NEED THE SANCTUARY OF OUR GARDENS — THEY ARE THE BRIDGE THAT ALLOWS US TO FIND OUR SPIRITUAL SELVES, AGAIN AND AGAIN.

THERE IS SOMETHING JOYOUSLY MEDITATIVE ABOUT SPENDING TIME AMONG NATURE. THE GRANDEUR OF THE TREES, THE DIVERSITY OF COLOUR PROVIDED BY THE FLORA AND THE HEADY SCENT OF LIFE GROWING ALL AROUND, CONSTITUTE A REMINDER THAT ALL WE NEED TO NURTURE AND SOOTHE OUR SOULS IS OFFERED BY MOTHER EARTH HERSELF. ALTHOUGH IT MAY NOT SEEM LIKE THE MOST OBVIOUS FIRST PORT OF CALL WHEN LOOKING FOR DECORATING INSPIRATION, THE WILDNESS OF NATURE TAMED INTO A BEAUTIFUL, WELL-THOUGHT-OUT GARDEN CAN POSSESS SOME OF THE MOST EXCITING EXAMPLES OF CREATIVE ABUNDANCE AND SPATIAL CONSIDERATION THAT YOU CAN FIND. YOU ONLY NEED TO TAKE A WALK THROUGH YOUR LOCAL BOTANICAL GARDEN TO SEE THAT A GARDEN'S STRUCTURE IS AS IMPORTANT AS THE GREENERY AND FLOWERS THAT FILL IT.

HUMANS HAVE ALWAYS SOUGHT TO MOULD AND DESIGN THE VASTNESS OF NATURE, DISSECTING LARGER SPACES INTO SMALLER VIGNETTES, IN MUCH THE SAME WAY THAT WE SHAPE CLAY IN SCULPTURE OR FORM CONCRETE INTO BUILDINGS. YOUR RESPONSE TO DIFFERENT STYLES OF GARDEN — FOR EXAMPLE, WHETHER IT IS DISSECTED BY CLEARLY DEFINED BORDERS OR ALLOWED TO GROW IN A MORE ORGANIC, FLUID WAY; THE CHOICE OF PLANTS THAT FORM THE DECORATION — WILL GIVE YOU SOME INSIGHT INTO THE TYPES OF SPACES THAT YOU PREFER.

I LOVE SLIGHTLY WILD-LOOKING, UNREFINED GARDENS, THOSE THAT LOOK LIKE THEY HAVE GROWN SLOWLY AND ORGANICALLY OVER TIME. THESE GARDENS OFTEN APPEAR TO POSSESS LITTLE OBVIOUS SENSE OF ORDER. THEY ARE USUALLY FILLED WITH A MÉLANGE OF COLOUR AND FORM, WHICH SOMEHOW, DESPITE THEIR UNTAMED CHARACTERISTICS, SEEM TO HANG TOGETHER AS UNIFIED AND INSPIRING SPACES. IF YOU ARE AWARE OF THE IMPRESSIONIST ARTIST MONET'S GARDEN IN GIVERNY, FRANCE — THAT BEAUTIFUL PLACE THAT APPEARS IN SO MANY OF HIS ARTWORKS — YOU'LL GET A SENSE OF WHAT I MEAN. I'D LIKE TO THINK THAT MY APPROACH TO INTERIOR DESIGN AND DECORATING WORKS IN MUCH THE SAME WAY AS THE DESIGN OF THIS BEAUTIFUL GARDEN (ALTHOUGH MONET WOULD PROBABLY TURN IN HIS GRAVE AT THE IDEA). COMBINING SEEMINGLY DISPARATE COLOURS AND OBJECTS WITH CONTRASTING FORMS, AND STITCHING THEM TOGETHER WITH A THREAD OF BALANCE AND ORDER, IS MY IDEAL AESTHETIC. THESE SPACES

INSPIRATIONAL ELEMENTS:
LUSH
PRETTY
FLORAL
HEAVENLY

POSSESS JUST ENOUGH ORGANIZATION TO MAKE LIVING BEARABLE, BUT HAVE LOTS OF SURPRISES THROWN IN TO STIMULATE THE SENSES AND KEEP ALL WHO LIVE AMONG IT ON THEIR TOES.

THAT'S JUST ME. YOU, ON THE OTHER HAND, MAY PREFER A MORE ORDERED GARDEN, ONE WITH BOX HEDGES, MONOTONE FLORA, CLEAN LINES AND CLEARLY DEFINED SPACES, WHICH MIGHT INDICATE YOUR DESIRE FOR A CALMER, MORE CONTEMPORARY FLAVOUR IN YOUR INTERIOR. ALTERNATIVELY, YOU MAY BE FOND OF NATIVE PLANTING: THE MUTED TONES OF INDIGENOUS FLORA AND THE ROUGH TEXTURE OF THE EARTH IN WHICH THEY ARE FOUND COULD BE THE LEAD THAT YOU ARE LOOKING FOR WHEN DECIDING THE INTERIOR PALETTE THAT YOU BEST RESPOND TO. IT'S IMPORTANT TO LOOK IN MANY DIFFERENT PLACES WHEN DRAWING ON INTERIOR INSPIRATION. ALTHOUGH IT MIGHT NOT BE THE MOST OBVIOUS SOURCE OF REVELATION, YOU MAY FIND THAT IT IS A GARDEN THAT PROVIDES THE CLEAREST INSIGHT INTO WHAT TYPES OF SPACES SUIT AN HONEST SENSE OF HOW YOU NEED TO LIVE.

collections I mentioned in the first chapter how important our collections are in conveying a true sense of who we are and how we like to live in our homes.

For me, it is the things that we gather, often subconsciously, that can give us the greatest insight into the types of decoration that we prefer and the things that we most love to live with. Generally, we build our collections over time, gathering slowly and in a way that reflects our travels through different experiences and places. We assemble pieces that ultimately tell the story of who we are and where we have come from. When I walk into a person's home I am affected by every aspect of it — from the architecture to the choice of sofa, curtaining and so forth — but it is the collections that line the shelves and every little nook and cranny that tell me the most about the person who lives there. That is because each element of our collections is usually acquired as a response from the heart rather than from the head, unless of course that particular collection fulfils a certain practical need.

It makes sense, then, to use your collections as a decorating tool when aiming to develop individuality in your home. After all, this is the element that can convey your sense of style better than anything else. My collection of ceramics, and to a lesser degree, my glassware, brings the widest smile to my face. Although I have only a small collection (at the moment), I feel these pieces reflect my life's journey the most honestly.

Don't worry if you have no collections — we all have to begin somewhere. Think about the types of things that reflect who you are and what you love. It could be that a series of 1960s Pop Art posters are what says the most about you. Or your collections of antique mirrors that you group together on one wall. Perhaps blown glass does it for you, with a collision of colour and texture lining every spare space. A wall of Aboriginal artwork may represent your love of Australian native culture. Or embroidered wall hangings may say the most about you. Whatever your loves are, don't be afraid to let them loose. Surround yourself in the things that speak to you and the experience of living will be more fulfilling for you.

OUR COLLECTIONS COMMUNICATE THE INNER WORKINGS OF OUR LIFE MOST CLEARLY; THEY REMIND US WHERE WE HAVE BEEN AND WHERE WE ARE GOING.

DISPLAY

Although you may have a large collection of treasures that are crying out to be released from storage, you could be holding back from unleashing them into the general scheme of your interior because of the difficulty that the element of display presents. And so, a couple of pointers are in order.

Ornaments

Grouping your ornaments in colour themes achieves the most effective display in a space. Solid greens, blues, reds and yellows will sit most happily together when they are positioned alongside their varying colour nuances. Throw in a patterned piece that partners well with the dominant colour that you are using. For example, if your collections are mostly blue, the pattern should have blue as its predominant base colour.

Choose ornaments that are well proportioned in relation to one another. An oversized vase, for example, will overshadow a small teacup and saucer when they are sitting together. Make sure that the nooks where the pieces will reside are well proportioned relative to the piece itself. A large sculpture will overwhelm a small box cube; a small vase will be dwarfed on a large sweep of shelf if it is left there to live alone. Keep period pieces together in one group if you are nervous about mixing and matching. Otherwise, mix styles but ensure that the colour palette in each period is complementary to the next. Although glass cabinets provide for a dust-free ornament, I like to keep my collections out — on tables, shelves and the like — enabling me to interact with them whenever my heart desires.

Framed art

Investing in artwork, particularly when it is original, is such a satisfying decorating tool — not just because artwork brings a space to life from a decorating point of view, but also because the story behind the work adds a certain atmosphere and energy that is carried within the work itself. When we choose artwork we generally make our decisions based on

[SENSE**OFSTYLESPACE**]

GROUPING COLLECTIONS TOGETHER, WITH A UNIFORMITY OF COLOUR, FORM, SCALE OR THEME, WORKS TO FORM, THE CHARACTER OF A ROOM.

how the piece looks to the eye — its colour, form and texture — but in fact it is the story behind the artwork that can have the most profound effect on us. Be sure when you purchase to ask for information about who created the piece and the message they want to convey through their work. Does that message sit with your vision? Do you like the story? All of these factors will ultimately affect how you like living with the artwork.

If you are lucky enough to have a bountiful art collection, grouping your artwork can often be a daunting task. Again, proportion plays a key role when you are making your decisions. Look at the artwork against the wall that you intend to hang it on. Does it sit well, or is it oversized for the space? Get a friend to hold it up for you so that you can get a good sense of it before you go knocking nails into walls. Smaller artworks can be grouped by artist or colour. If there is no commonality to the pieces that you own, lay them out on the floor in front of you and play with their positioning for a while. Move them around until you are satisfied that they are balanced and at ease with one another. A good pointer is to cut some newspaper into the shapes of your artworks and with reusable adhesive like Blu-Tac fasten them to the walls arranged as you intend to hang them. Arrange and rearrange until you feel comfortable with how the group sits together.

Wall hangings

There is nothing that I love more than seeing fabric hangings gracing the walls of a home. It is such a lovely way to add texture, pattern and dimension to a wall without having to paint it on or invest in original artwork. Choose your wall hangings as you would any other element of decoration — because you love what you see. However, if a large hanging is the most prominent feature in a room, ensure that the colour palette is reflective of or at least complementary to the palette in the rest of your furnishings. Hang your fabric from a simple pleat or add a natural, organic flavour to a room by pinning it to a branch or piece of bamboo. Pulling it over a frame to create a clean, geometric shape works well in a contemporary interior. For a lovely, rustic feel in your home, take your patchwork quilts off the bed and enjoy them as you would any piece of art.

your space

AND SO, HERE WE ARE – AT THE END OF OUR DECORATING JOURNEY TOGETHER, BUT AT THE BEGINNING OF YOUR SEARCH FOR INDIVIDUAL STYLE.

If you've made it this far, hopefully you will have gained some insight into who you are and how you like to live; into the types of environments that best suit you; and into the colours, patterns, forms and details that provide you with a sense of comfort in your home. Although space can be a daunting subject to tackle — it is such a large, even overwhelming, concept at times — when you do come to terms with how you feel about your space, it is easier to make style decisions that reflect an honest sense of who you are. Don't be afraid to connect with your instincts when making your decorating choices, it is the tool that you can rely on more than anything else to guide you in the right direction. And try to have a good time with it all. Creating is supposed to be fun — so don't be too hard on yourself in the process. You are creating an interior that suits you, after all, and so there is nobody else to impress but yourself. Most importantly, take your time and do your research; put your feet up for a while and reflect on your actions and choices as you go. There's no need to hurry. You have a lifetime to develop exactly the type of interior that you want, so take your time. And watch your space evolve with you.

THE DECORATION OF YOUR HOME IS AN OPPORTUNITY TO PUT YOURSELF ON DISPLAY, TO INTERACT DAILY WITH THE SYMBOLS OF THE LIFE YOU HAVE LIVED AND THE LOVES THAT YOU VALUE. IN THIS WAY, INTERIOR DECORATION GIVES US THE STRENGTH TO BE OURSELVES.

REALISTIC ILLUSIONIST ART HAD DISSEMBLED THE MEDIUM USING ART TO CONCEAL ART MODERNISM USED ART TO CALL ATTENTION TO ART THE LIMITATIONS THAT CONSTITUTE THE MEDIUM OF PAINTING THE FLAT SURFACE THE SHAPE OF THE SUPPORT THE PROPERTIES OF PIGMENT WERE TREATED BY THE OLD MASTERS AS NEGATIVE FACTORS THAT COULD BE ACKNOWLEDGED ONLY IMPLICITLY OR INDIRECTLY MODERNIST PAINTING HAS COME TO REGARD THESE SAME LIMITATIONS AS POSITIVE FACTORS THAT ARE TO BE ACKNOWLEDGED OPENLY MANETS PAINTINGS BECAME THE FIRST MODERNIST ONES BY VIRTUE OF THE FRANKNESS WITH WHICH THEY DECLARED THE SURFACES ON WHICH THEY WERE PAINTED THE IMPRESSIONISTS IN MANETS WAKE ABJURED UNDERPAINTING AND GLAZING TO LEAVE THE EYE UNDER NO DOUBT AS TO THE FACT THAT THE COLORS USED WERE MADE OF REAL PAINT THAT CAME FROM POTS OR TUBES CEZANNE SACRIFICED VERISIMILITUDE OR CORRECTNESS IN ORDER TO FIT DRAWING AND DESIGN MORE EXPLICITLY TO THE RECTANGULAR SHAPE OF THE CANVAS IT WAS THE STRESSING HOWEVER OF THE INELUCTABLE FLATNESS OF THE SUPPORT THAT REMAINED MOST FUNDAMENTAL IN THE PROCESSES BY WHICH PICTORIAL ART CRITICIZED AND DEFINED ITSELF UNDER M

index

A

ABC Carpet and Home
  (New York) 33
alcoves 117, 132
alfresco spaces 102-5
ambience 17, 33
art 61-2, 154-5
atmosphere 10

B

backdrop, for life 10
backdrop colours 133-4
balance 110, 113, 117
balconies 103-4
barbecues 95
Barbie 122
Barcelona 120
bathing 68
bathrooms 68-71, 134
  colour choice 71
  lighting 71
bed linen 87, 143-4
bedrooms 84-7, 142
  decoration 87
  environment 85-6
beds 85
  mattress 87
blue 23, 41, 69, 81, 140-1, 151
  and calm 59
blunders 43
books 4, 101, 145
bookstores 88-90
breathing space 24, 29
busyness 110, 117

C

candlelight 59, 71, 127
carpeting 100, 147
chairs 31, 42, 73, 79-80
cities 26-7, 103, 119-20
cleansing spaces 68-71
clutter 67, 82
  see also stuff
cocktails 95

cocoons 14, 52, 130
collections 38-41, 75, 152-5
  displaying 154-5
  see also framed art
colour
  as backdrop 133-4
  bathrooms 71
  character of 9
  communal spaces 53
  in details 134
  for entertaining 95
  sacred spaces 59
  work spaces 66, 67
colour schemes 132-5
  three-part process 135
communal living spaces 50-3,
  108
  colour choices 53
  layout 52
  patterns for 53
concrete, tinted 70
cooking 95
  outdoors 104
Copenhagen 120
countryside 18, 20-2
  colours of 22, 59
creative process 10
creativity 9, 29, 61
  and clutter 67
  defined 117
crowds 50

D

daydreaming 24, 29, 75
design elements 9, 10, 108-9
Designers Guild 53
desires 29, 46
dining rooms 11, 80, 94-5
dual-purpose rooms 87, 117

E

eateries 78, 93-4, 128-30
eating spaces 76-9
  decoration 79

emporiums 32-5
energy 10, 36
entertaining spaces 92-5
  colour 95
  layout 94
  outdoor 94, 95, 104
entrance areas 99, 100
environment
  at odds with 18
  effects of 46, 49
experimentation 43, 109

F

fabric 137, 143
feature walls 134
feng shui 58
floor plans 113, 122
floorboards 147
fluorescent lights 125, 127
food 76, 78
foundations 109, 133
foyers 99
framed art, displaying 1, 38, 51,
  100, 106, 145, 154-5, 157
framework, of life 14
furniture, arranging 52-3, 58, 94,
  113, 122

G

galleries 60-2
garden sheds 72
gardens 56, 94, 104, 148-50
glassware 41, 95, 152
green 128, 131, 153
  and calm 59

H

hallways 99, 100, 124
halogen lights 127
hoarding 82
hobbies 72, 75
home 8-9, 14, 152
home office 64, 65, 72
homeware shops 33

hotels 99
human interaction 50, 93

I

illumination *see* lighting
illusions 117, 134
imagination 24, 154
individuality 8-9, 49, 114, 134
inspiration 22, 120, 129, 149
inspiration file 34, 43
instinct 36, 156

K

kitchens 12, 16, 52, 53, 76-9, 116
knick-knacks 39-40, 152-5

L

L-shaped rooms 117
lamp lighting 127
libraries 56
light 86
    natural patterns 125
    too much/too little 114, 126
lighting 124-7
    bathrooms 71
    character of 9
    in dual-purpose rooms 117
    with lamps 127
    and mood 71, 125-6, 130
    sacred spaces 59
living rooms 52-3

M

meditation 58
mirrors 152
mood boards 34, 43

N

nature 59, 103, 104, 149
needs 29, 46
New York 33, 119, 120

O

odd spaces 114-17, 132
open-plan rooms 36, 53, 96
orange 53, 71

ornaments 154
outdoor spaces 102-5

P

paint 79
    metallic 147
    textured 147
parties 93, 94
pattern 135
    bedrooms 84, 87, 136
    communal spaces 53
patterning 136-9
    and balance 138
pergolas 104
photographs 40, 120
pink 53
possessions 39-40
private spaces 72-5
    comfort 75
    see also sacred spaces
proportion 9

Q

quiet spaces 56-9

R

red 53, 132, 153
Red Ginger (Byron Bay) 33
relaxing 29, 58, 68, 71, 108
rugs 51, 100
rural spaces 18, 20-2

S

sacred spaces 56-9, 108
    colour 59
    energy 58
    lighting 59
screens 57, 115
self-abandonment 109, 134
self-discovery 10, 29, 156
shopping 33-4
sketches 113, 122
sleep 85, 87
small spaces 117
soul food 56, 71, 103
space 156
    defined 10

layout 110-13
    nature of 9
spaces
    assessing 30, 46, 110
    controlling 14
    defining 14
    for living 6
    moving through 14, 22, 36, 100
    responding to 36, 43
stairways 37, 101
stonework 147
storage 82-3
streetscapes 18, 26-7, 118-20
stuff 39-40, 152-5
style 34, 40, 53, 139

T

tableware 79, 95
texture 129, 143-4
tilework 70, 78-9, 134
touch, sense of 143-4
tranquillity 59
transitional spaces 98-101
tribal patterns 137-8

W

wall hangings 152, 155
wall tiles 134
wallpaper, textured 147
wallpapering 134
walls 110
wet areas 134
white 12, 28, 92, 112
    and clinical 71
    and food 79
    light-reflective 114, 126
    and tranquillity 59
wood flooring 147
working spaces 64-7
    colour for 66, 67
    storage systems 66

Y

yellow 53

Published by Murdoch Books Pty Limited

Murdoch Books Pty Limited Australia

Pier 8/9, 23 Hickson Road, Millers Point NSW 2000

Phone: + 61 (0) 2 8220 2000 Fax: + 61 (0) 2 8220 2558

Website: www.murdochbooks.com.au

Murdoch Books UK Limited

Erico House, 6th Floor

93–99 Upper Richmond Road, Putney, London SW15 2TG

Phone: + 44 (0) 20 8785 5995 Fax: + 44 (0) 20 8785 5985

Chief Executive: Juliet Rogers
Publishing Director: Kay Scarlett

Editor: Diana Hill
Concept and design: Lauren Camilleri
Production Manager: Tiffany Johnson

National Library of Australia

Cataloguing-in-Publication Data:

Fricke, Shannon.

Sense of style: Space

Includes index. ISBN 978 1 74045 831 3.

1. Space (Architecture). 2. Interior decoration.

3. Lifestyles. I. Title. 720.1

Printed by 1010 International Limited.

Printed in China